befor

during

after

I also got dividend in hospital

HAPPY B-DAY

I spent my birthday in hospital and a little party and most of my friends on the ward came!

Soon I could walk . . . .

Playroom →

Hospital

When I am grown up I want to be a nurse at Great Ormond Street. It is the best hospital.

Great ormond Street Saved my life and I will always remember them for it ♡

The remarkable story of
Great Ormond Street Hospital

Kevin Telfer

SIMON &
SCHUSTER

London · New York · Sydney · Toronto

Great Ormond Street Hospital would like to give enormous thanks to the following organisations and individuals for their generous support in the making of this book:

Anshen + Allen, Samuel French, Gardiner & Theobald LLP, Oxford University Press, Caspar and Kate Rock, Michael Simkins LLP.

Without this support the production of 'The remarkable story of Great Ormond Street Hospital' would not have been possible.

This book is dedicated to all the children treated at Great Ormond Street Hospital and their families.

First published in Great Britain by Simon & Schuster UK Ltd. 2008
A CBS Company

Simon & Schuster UK Ltd
Africa House
64-78 Kingsway
London
WC2B 6AH

1 3 5 7 9 10 8 6 4 2

Design and text editing: Calcium
Picture research: Kevin Telfer and Nick Baldwin
Printed and bound in China

ISBN 9781847371133 hardback
ISBN 9781847371140 paperback

All photographs are © Great Ormond Street Hospital and Great Ormond Street Children's Charity apart from the following images which have been reproduced by kind permission:

AFP/Getty Images p.119; Alex Brown p.165; Andy Lane p.121-123; Brett Williams p.95, 99; Cecil Beaton Studio Archive, Sothebys p.117; Charles Dickens Museum p.13, 133; Daily Herald, Daily Illustrated, Daily Mirror and Odham's Press, reproduced by Mirrorpix p.55, 76, 110, 111, 112, 113, 114, 115, 118, 157; David Bailey p.72; David Wyatt p.114; Duncan Raban p.32, 178, back cover; © Edmund Sumner/View with kind assistance from and Anshen + Allen p.172, 187, 188, 189; Janine Goulding p.66-67; Jefferson Smith p.186; John Swannell/Camera Press London p.5; Kevin Telfer p.73; Kipper Williams p.145; Leanne Pannell p.101; Llewelyn Davies Yeang p.195-196; MarcusLyon.com p.96-97; Martin Lupton p.163; Mary Evans Picture Library p.19, 21, 24, 30; Piers Cavendish p.156; Robert Ingpen and Palazzo Editions Ltd p.6; Royal College of Physicians p.51; Sven Arnstein p.101; Wellcome Institute p.87; Western Daily Press p.200.

CONTENTS

BUCKINGHAM PALACE

MESSAGE FROM THE QUEEN

When Queen Victoria became Patron of Great Ormond Street Hospital on its foundation, it was the first institution in the United Kingdom to provide specialist in-patient care to children only. Today, though the challenges may be different, Great Ormond Street Hospital continues to be at the forefront of paediatric provision and research into child health.

Many of the illnesses which were a threat to the children of 1852 are thankfully no longer considered serious by the standards of the 21st Century. Nevertheless, for the thousands of patients who are treated each year by the hospital's doctors, nurses and healthcare assistants, the care offered by Great Ormond Street Hospital is of the utmost importance. This treatment might include kidney transplants, heart surgery, operations for brain tumours and gene therapy. Many of these great advances would not have been possible without the work of the hospital's research body, the UCL Institute of Child Health.

Throughout its long history, countless children, and their families, have had cause to be thankful for the dedication and expertise they have encountered at Great Ormond Street Hospital. Many more will doubtless have similar cause in the future. As Patron of Great Ormond Street Hospital for Children, I am full of admiration for the way in which it has, for over a century and a half, remained true to its motto – 'The child first and always'. It is a noble endeavour, as this book amply illustrates.

Elizabeth R

May 2007

The Queen's official golden jubilee photograph from 2002, a copy of which was presented to Great Ormond Street Hospital in the same year, when it was celebrating its 150th anniversary. The Queen, as patron of the hospital, has visited it in the years of her coronation, silver jubilee and golden jubilee

4

A parent's introduction
by Lee Elliot Major

'I'm youth, I'm joy!'
Peter Pan

At 9 pm on 13 August 2003, our newborn son arrived by ambulance at Great Ormond Street Hospital. The best day of our lives had turned into our worst nightmare. Little did we know it was all a blessing in disguise. Jack, we were to find out, had a rare condition called Hirschsprung's disease – critically, part of his bowel was not working. Perhaps Jack might not be with us now if it were not for the expertise that greeted him at the hospital.

During our time at the hospital we met doctors from every corner of the world; each managed somehow to be leading-edge academic, medical practitioner, science communicator and social worker all in one. It is these doctors, and the nurses, administrators and other staff that make the hospital such a national and international treasure of modern medicine.

The legendary Professor Lewis Spitz led the team who operated on two-month-old Jack. Who else could I trust more to undertake such a task? Now I look at the fading scar on Jack's tummy and marvel at the fine handiwork of those surgeons.

In Peter Pan the hospital found its perfect patron. British author JM Barrie left the copyright of his book to Great Ormond Street Hospital; fittingly it will for ever be linked with the boy who never grows up. 'I'm youth, I'm joy,' Peter proclaims. Great Ormond Street Hospital is a happy place. Unwell children, unlike adults, do not tend to feel sorry for themselves.

The hospital, too, will, in one sense, never grow up. Children get better and leave to become adults; others, tragically, are destined to stay young for ever. But these are not 'lost' children, like Peter's motley crew. As one former patient, now a proud grandmother, says in this book, she was made by staff to feel normal. For us, it was a home from home.

As a parent at the hospital you cannot help but be affected by the beautiful and brave child patients. They helped us to feel human again. Far too many of us in our busy lives sever all links with childhood – and lose touch with the things that really matter.

I also believe you judge a society by how well it cares for its most vulnerable – those who cannot help themselves, particularly those with most of their lives ahead of them.

We know now that Jack was one of many thousands of patients treated in 2003, and one of several million who have been helped since the hospital opened as a single, ten-bed ward more than a century and a half ago.

The journey of the hospital has not always been an easy one, as this book shows, but it has always had an ability to adapt and overcome adversity. For it to prosper in the future, the hospital must continue to evolve and renew itself. I am sure it will. The real fairytale is that parents and patients will continue to be blessed, as we have been, for many, many years to come.

Peter Pan has offered hope and inspiration to thousands of sick children at the hospital for more than 150 years. Illustration by Robert Ingpen from Peter Pan and Wendy *(2004, Templar Publishing)*

Patients at the hospital were invited to enter a competition in which they told their stories.

8-and-under winners: Milly Pyne and Louis Tavare

Milly has Crouzon's Syndrome, which causes facial deformity and can create pressure on the brain. She was operated on by craniofacial surgeon Mr David Dunaway. After the successful surgery she wore a frame on her head, which gradually moved her face forward to lessen the symptoms of her condition. Milly tells her story below.

I was born in 1998 in Kendal, Cumbria.

I went to Great Ormond Street Hospital.

My ward is called Tiger Ward.

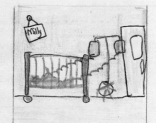

I had my first operation when I was a baby.

The nurses on Tiger Ward are all my friends. I like them and they play with me.

In March 2007 I had a big operation and I had to have a RED frame fitted by Prof and Mr. D.

When I am grown up I want to be a nurse at Great Ormond Street. It is the best hospital.

L ouis Tavare was diagnosed with Burkitt's Lymphoma, a very rare form of cancer. His cartoon describes, as he puts it, 'the beginning of hell to the end', during which he had to undergo many injections and blood tests, as well as the side effects of chemotherapy, including his hair loss. His story ends on a positive note, however, with a picture of Louis saying 'I'm back!' He promises a sequel entitled 'The resurrection of the bad berc!'

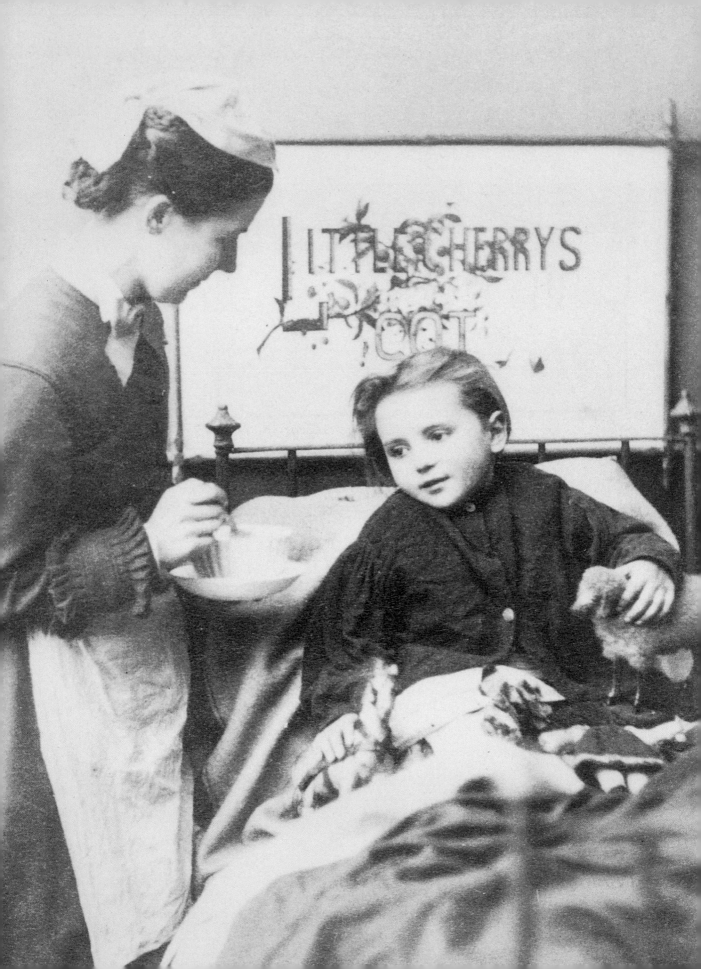

Chapter 1

Beginnings

'Enlarged sympathy with children was one of the chief contributions made by the Victorian English to real civilisation.'
GM Trevelyan

In comparison with the older general hospitals in Britain, Great Ormond Street Hospital itself could be considered a child. The idea and spirit of youth is completely apt for a hospital that has cared for 'the child first and always', to use the words of its own motto, for more than 150 years, making it the oldest children's hospital in the English-speaking world. The hospital's motto, as well as being a code of practice, is a celebration of childhood and all that it stands for. This particular 'child' has been so exuberant in its development, though, that it has regularly outgrown the buildings that house it, and has frequently required larger and better structures – a challenge that continues today. And it is that same youthful exuberance of fast-paced change that is so evident in its rich history, a history that is also a fascinating journey through medicine and society from the 1850s to the present day. A check on the current state of the health of Great Ormond Street Hospital shows that its youthfulness remains (perhaps, like its friend Peter Pan, it is a child that refuses to grow up). Its evolving forms of pioneering treatment and need for new models of care call for significant new development. This healthy, precocious child, one of the top children's hospitals in the world, still has much more to achieve.

A Victorian nurse treats a child. Childhood came to be viewed as an icon of hope and optimism during the Victorian era. With this newfound vision also came an interest in the health and welfare of children

A timely birth

How did Great Ormond Street Hospital come to be born? Its beginnings are firmly rooted in their time, and are linked with important figures such as its founder, Dr Charles West, and its most celebrated early benefactor and formidable champion, Charles Dickens.

Perhaps surprisingly, before the birth of The Hospital for Sick Children in Great Ormond Street in 1852 (which only officially became known as Great Ormond Street Hospital for Children in 1994), there was no hospital in Britain with dedicated inpatient facilities for children. Even the large general hospitals did not have separate wards for children. Nonetheless, a survey in 1843 found that only 136 children under the age of ten were being treated in general hospitals in London – at that time the largest city in the world with a population of more than 2 million people. Britain was lagging behind its European counterparts in this respect, as many of the larger European cities did have children's hospitals by 1850. The first was opened in Paris in 1802.

An urbanising society

British society in the mid-19th century was undergoing massive change – industrialisation swept the country and population growth accelerated. The population more than trebled between 1800 and 1900, from 10 million to 32 million. It also became increasingly concentrated in urban areas. This urbanisation brought numerous social problems, principally poverty and its attendant symptoms of poor health and malnutrition. In such a rapidly growing population, children inevitably formed a higher percentage of it than they do today. During this time, children under 14 years never formed less than 40 per cent of the population, compared to approximately 20 per cent today.

Children in the spotlight

This situation also led to an increased focus on the role that children played in society. This can be seen most famously in the work of Charles Dickens, as well as other novelists, who began to use childhood as a significant theme in their fiction. Many famous literary works of the 19th century are about children, such as *Oliver Twist*,

In the early days, most of the hospital's patients came from 'slum' districts within a short walking distance. One of these was Saffron Hill in Clerkenwell, as seen in this photograph from around the turn of the 20th century

The author Charles Dickens not only raised enormous sums of money for the hospital, but also eloquently argued the case for a children's hospital as an innovation that was urgently needed in London

The author Charles Dickens not only raised enormous sums of money for the hospital, but also eloquently argued the case for a children's hospital as an innovation that was urgently needed in London

Vulnerable children

Although children across the world today remain vulnerable, without doubt in the British society of 1850 children had less formal protection and there were fewer opportunities for their welfare. The poorest children, in particular, suffered enormously from deprivation and various forms of exploitation, such as extremely hard, dangerous and poorly paid work. Examples included factory and mine work, and chimney sweeping.

Alice's Adventures in Wonderland and *Jane Eyre*. Dickens, who was to play such a crucial role in the early days of the hospital, created a whole raft of child characters, such as Tiny Tim, Little Nell, Pip and David Copperfield.

European, and particularly British, views of childhood were changing in the 19th century. Whereas previously children had been seen as rather fragile, miniature adults, in whom it was unwise to invest too much, now there was an emerging awareness of childhood as a special time, not merely a transition between infancy and adulthood but a stage of life with its own particular value. Children were popularised and sentimentalised as symbols of innocence and goodness; Dickens, for instance, wrote that they were 'fresh from God'.

Dickens was probably the most prodigious chronicler of the conditions in which many of those children lived. He based much of his writing on observations taken from the areas of central London close to Great Ormond Street. When he first became famous, in the late 1830s, Dickens was living just a couple of hundred metres from where the hospital would later be sited. The 'dark, threatening and contaminated city' of London that Dickens saw then was a dangerous place.

Tiny Tim in Dickens's Christmas Carol *became one of the most enduring images of a sick child*

There were regular outbreaks of epidemics, such as the typhus epidemic of 1847 that infected half a million people – a quarter of the population of London. Peter Ackroyd describes the city as a place where 'adults and children died of malnutrition and disease, where open sewers and cesspools spread their miasma into the foggy air, where it took only the shortest period to turn off one of the grand thoroughfares or respectable streets of the city and enter a landscape of filth and destitution, death and misery'. Near Great Ormond Street there were a number of such areas: some of the most infamous and wretched slums in London, such as Seven Dials off Shaftesbury Avenue and Saffron Hill in Clerkenwell, were only a short walk away. It is estimated that the mortality rate for babies in these poverty-stricken areas was 50 per cent. Today that figure is more like 0.5 per cent.

A new hospital

It was clear that something needed to be done to alleviate the suffering of so many of London's children at that time. But there was no clear consensus that the founding of a hospital was the right thing to do. One man, however, Dr Charles West, had the thorough conviction that it was.

West had been campaigning for a number of years to found a children's hospital in the capital. Until 1850 his efforts had been continually hindered by opposition that took a number of different forms. One of the strongest arguments against a children's hospital was that putting a lot of sick children together in one building would only increase the likelihood of outbreaks of infection. This would seem to have been backed up by the high mortality rates at the Hôpital des Enfants Malades in Paris, the oldest institution of its kind, which was also commonly criticised for having a poor standard of nursing. However, an example far closer to home was also being used to oppose the idea of a children's hospital. The Foundling Hospital was just a stone's throw away from Great Ormond Street. It was actually an orphanage rather than a hospital, founded in 1746 by a retired sea captain called Thomas Coram. Coram had set up the orphanage after seeing large numbers of babies either dead or dying in the London streets. In the first four years 14,934 babies were admitted, but only 4,545 survived, less

Dr Charles West – a portrait

Dr Charles West, the founder of Great Ormond Street Hospital, was a driven, pioneering man. Numerous accounts suggest this also made him not always the easiest person to get on with. He had to work exceptionally hard to transform his vision of a children's hospital in London into reality. But he also had to battle throughout his life against prejudice, initially to his being the son of a Baptist preacher, which at that time meant he was unable to go to Oxford or Cambridge university, and later to his conversion to Catholicism. Catholics were widely discriminated against in Victorian Britain, and West often found his way impeded. Had he not been Catholic, it seems likely that he would have achieved even more success in what was nonetheless an extremely accomplished life. Understanding these factors is essential in trying to understand West; the fact that he faced – and largely overcame – such pressure, adversity and prejudice over so many years says a lot about the type of man he was.

Charles West was born in 1816, and began his education at his father's school. At the age of fifteen he began his involvement with medicine when he was apprenticed to Mr Gray, an apothecary (similar to a modern-day pharmacist) in Amersham who had once worked at St George's Hospital, London. He then went to St Bartholomew's Hospital (Bart's) in London, where he was an outstanding student, winning the prize for medicine in 1834 and first prize for midwifery and forensic science in 1835. As he was ineligible for Oxford or Cambridge, he decided to attend Bonn University. His European odyssey was to prove highly instructive for him, both medically and for his personal accomplishments: he spoke a number of European languages and had friends across the continent. So perhaps in this instance the prejudices of his age yielded some benefit. He was a prize winner again at Bonn, before he arrived in Paris in 1836, where a children's hospital had already been in operation for more than 30 years. He subsequently travelled to Berlin, where he acquired his doctorate.

He was back in London by 1839, where he worked at Bart's and served at the Dispensary for Children in Waterloo Road. He was appointed physician at the latter in 1842. He secured more appointments through the 1840s, first as a lecturer in midwifery and then as a physician accoucheur (obstetrician) at the Middlesex Hospital and lecturer in midwifery at Bart's. His lectures were published as a book, *Lectures on Diseases and Childhood*, in 1848 and were a great success, being widely translated and printed in seven editions. One reviewer described his book as 'standing by itself upon its important subject, in our language – unapproached – unrivalled'.

All this time, West was striving to turn the Waterloo Road dispensary into a children's hospital with inpatient facilities, though in large part the 'jealousy of local medical men', who presumably felt the new institution would be a threat to their private practice, meant that his efforts failed. West felt snubbed and highly dissatisfied with Bart's where he had been appointed honorary physician accoucheur, with responsibility for the care of patients, but without the prestige of having his own beds. His name was also excluded from the list of hospital medical officers in the annual reports. He was said to be unpopular at the hospital, no doubt the result of incidents such as the argument with surgeons that occurred when he said that, apart from one eminent surgeon, the staff were not competent to perform the operations on his ward.

The foundation of the Hospital for Sick Children at Great Ormond Street, then, gave him huge satisfaction. 'The one dream of my life has been to see the children's hospital well established,' he said, 'and that done I do not know that there is anything left for me to wish for'. But despite achieving his dream, there would be numerous and bitter arguments between West and others involved in the running of the hospital. The fact that he handed in his resignation in 1854, after just two years, provides a taste of what was to come. His resignation was not accepted, but West's strong views and apparent inability to compromise led to frequent disputes, as hospital policy veered in different directions from his own ideas.

But West's strength of character manifested itself more compassionately in the holistic vision of care he had for his child patients, a vision that was significantly ahead of its time. In particular, he was committed to good nursing, and he wrote a booklet called *How to Nurse Sick Children* in 1854. Elizabeth Lomax wrote of it that, 'no detail was beneath his notice, for West could explain how to bath a small child, to apply leeches or a cold pack, prop up a child with difficulty in breathing and even how best to amuse small patients by reading, singing, rocking or with stories, "tell them of your own childhood", for "all children love to hear what happened to grown people when they were young".'

West retired from active service at Great Ormond Street Hospital in February 1875. He died in 1898 at the age of eighty-two.

Unlike many of the eminent physicians and surgeons from the first fifty years of Great Ormond Street Hospital, West was not knighted, possibly because of his faith or perhaps due to his argumentative nature. He said late in life that, 'there are two things for which I care very much. The one is the welfare of the Children's Hospital to which the energies of the best years of my life have been devoted. The other is that when I have passed away, those to whom my memory will still be dear may hear my name sometimes mentioned with a blessing, as that of the founder of the first children's hospital that ever existed in England'. In this his legacy is assured.

'The foundation of a hospital for sick children was the dream of my youth and the occupation of thirty years of manhood.' Charles West

than 30 per cent. The Foundling Hospital was also unpopular because many Victorian Britons felt that it encouraged licentious behaviour among the poor. A new hospital for sick children was similarly criticised in some quarters for encouraging irresponsibility among parents. Many also regarded it as unnatural that children should be separated from their parents while they underwent medical treatment.

Despite such discouragements, West was determined that the progress of medical science that he sought to promote, allied with resourceful management, could overcome the dangers of a high mortality rate at his hospital. As for the idea that children would better be treated at home, he could see that the often squalid conditions in deprived areas seemed actively to promote the incidence of serious epidemic diseases such as typhus, measles and scarlet fever. The advancement of medical science in itself was also going to be a key aim of any new institution, and West hoped that these advancements would enable doctors to provide better treatment for children in general, and ultimately improve the health of children throughout society.

Increased specialisation

The enormous increase of specialist hospitals in the 19th century was a remarkable phenomenon, the beginning of an increase in medical specialisation that continues today. The norm for physicians then was for generalisation: the theory was that this made them equally confident in treating any type of disease and illness. Surgeons, too, could perform facial surgery as readily as abdominal procedures. By the time Great Ormond Street Hospital was founded there were already five specialist hospitals for eye diseases, four for pulmonary diseases and three for orthopaedics. Specialisation was now seen as a way in which young doctors could make their mark on the profession, particularly those who were not favoured by birth and connections in high places.

West had travelled extensively in Europe and was aware of the many children's hospitals there. He realised that London must have such an institution if medicine in Britain was going to keep pace with developments abroad. But he also realised that specialisation was the only way in which detailed knowledge

Angela Burdett-Coutts was one of the country's most active philanthropists in the 19th century and gave her support to the hospital

of a particular area of medicine could realistically be achieved. This trajectory has continued ever since.

Services for children

There were dispensaries offering outpatient services for children. The first one opened at Red Lion Square in Holborn in 1769, just a few hundred metres from Great Ormond Street. West's experience of working at a similar dispensary on Waterloo Road, and his frustrated attempts to convert this into a fully fledged children's hospital, convinced him that he would need powerful patronage to help him achieve his aim.

In 1849 an introduction to a highly influential London doctor, Dr Henry Bence Jones, brought West a step closer to forming just such a distinguished group of patrons. Bence Jones was able to assemble a number of high-profile and wealthy supporters, including the wealthiest woman in England and perhaps the greatest philanthropist of the 19th century, Angela Burdett-Coutts. Also in the group were the widow of Lord Byron, Lady Noel Byron, and Lord Ashley, a prominent MP who promoted a number of parliamentary bills for the welfare of children and who later became the 7th Earl of Shaftesbury.

Dr Henry Bence Jones was instrumental in introducing the idea of a children's hospital to some of the most influential members of London society

The task begins

A first assembly of the nine men of the 'provisional committee' of the hospital, including West and Bence Jones, met at Bence Jones's house in Mayfair in January 1850 and set the crucial work in motion. In March the following year the first public meeting for the foundation of the hospital was chaired by Lord Ashley MP.

The site of the hospital had already been chosen by the time of this public meeting. Dickens later wrote of Great Ormond Street that, 'it is cut off now, from the life of the town – in London but not of it – a suburb left between the New Road and High Holborn'. It was away from the tumult, thrum and noise of the larger streets around it, a historical accident of town planning that still exerts its legacy today, making Great Ormond Street feel like an idyllic backwater in the centre of town: an ideal location for the peace and quiet needed to help sick children get better. The street was first laid out in the 1690s, during the period of immense construction that followed the Great Fire of London, and is almost certainly named after James Butler, the 1st Duke of Ormonde.

The first public meeting of the Hospital for Sick Children: a sketch

The elegant 18th-century Hanover Square Rooms were the venue for a 'public meeting held to promote the foundation of a children's hospital' on 18 March 1851. Just three months later Charles Dickens, who had a great love of theatre, put on public performances of Bulwer Lytton's play *Not So Bad As We Seem* in the same venue, with a number of his friends and associates in the cast, including fellow novelist Wilkie Collins and famous illustrator John Tenniel (the original illustrator of Lewis Carroll's *Alice's Adventures in Wonderland*). The set design for the play was by Joseph Paxton, truly the man of the moment in London at the time, as he had designed the spectacular Crystal Palace in Hyde Park for the Great Exhibition that was open between May and October of that year. The same play had been performed by the cast for the first time in front of Queen Victoria on 16 April. The Queen seems to have been suitably amused, writing in her diary: 'All acted on the whole well. Dickens (the celebrated author) admirably...The dresses and scenery were beautiful'. Queen Victoria, Tenniel, Carroll and Dickens were all ultimately to play some part themselves in the history of The Hospital for Sick Children.

Lord Ashley was a progressive legislator with a special interest in the welfare of children. He was chairman at the first public meeting of the hospital and in 1852 became the hospital's president

The public meeting, in the main an exercise in public relations and fundraising for the new hospital, was chaired by Lord Ashley MP, though he makes clear from the outset that he may not be able to remain at the meeting for long. 'You will I hope excuse me if I discharge the duties of the chair in a somewhat hurried manner,' he says, 'for I have just quitted another meeting, and I shall be obliged, in consequence of the adjournment in the debate in the House of Commons, to leave this meeting at a very early period.' Nonetheless, he obviously felt that the cause was of sufficient importance to impart some eloquence to the words he addressed to some distinguished members of London society present at the meeting, including the Bishop of London.

He goes on to say, 'I think I may bring to your recollection, if not to your knowledge, this fact; that in this great and wealthy metropolis, the greatest perhaps, and I have no doubt the wealthiest that ever yet existed on the face of the earth, there is no institution of the kind which it is now proposed to establish'.

The point that many other cities in Europe had hospitals for children, yet London – the pre-eminent world city at the time (at least in the eyes of Victorian Londoners) – did not, is emphasised by a number of speakers at the meeting. But the Earl of Carlisle, who spoke after Ashley, had a more direct appeal to the audience. 'Sick children!' he exclaims. 'Does not that combination carry its own reproof, and its own appeal with it?' His words anticipate those of Dickens when he wrote about the Hospital for Sick Children a year later. 'A sick child is a contradiction of ideas, like a cold summer. But to quench the summer in a child's heart is, thank God, not easy.'

The Earl of Carlisle MP, like Ashley, was also in something of a rush ('I happen unfortunately to have but very few minutes at my disposal'), but before he departed he made reference to some telling statistics. 'You cannot read the rate of infant mortality, you cannot read the ratio of those who perish in the earlier

HOSPITAL

FOR

SICK CHILDREN,

GREAT ORMOND STREET, QUEEN SQUARE.

REPORT

OF

PROCEEDINGS AT A PUBLIC MEETING,

HELD TO

Promote the Foundation of a Children's Hospital,

AT

THE HANOVER-SQUARE ROOMS,

March 18th, 1851.

THE RIGHT HON. LORD ASHLEY, M.P.,
IN THE CHAIR.

LONDON:
PRINTED BY BLADES, EAST, & BLADES, ABCHURCH LANE,
KING WILLIAM STREET.
—
1851.

*Funds raised from the first public meeting meant
that within a few months the hospital was able to
purchase its first premises on Great Ormond Street*

years of life, without being convinced that
many die who ought not; and if many die,
how many more must pine and languish?'
He also paid tribute to Ashley as a man who
had 'lived and laboured for the good of
others, and especially of the weak and
defenceless'. Indeed, as an MP for twenty-
five years and a noted philanthropist, Ashley
had promoted a number of welfare schemes
for children, and was to become president
of the hospital and remain so until his death.
After the Bishop of London had spoken,
Ashley gave his apologies and left the
meeting. The minutes record that, 'His
lordship retired amidst much cheering.'

Dr Burrows wanted to emphasise the
way in which the new hospital would
contribute to advances in medicine, saying
that at presents 'the student is instructed in
the theory of disease, and may attend a
course of lectures on the disease of children,
but the teacher who has given that course of
lectures is unable to give practical
illustrations.' He makes the point that there
are great distinctions to be made between
children and adults, and that a hospital

would provide useful opportunities for
doctors to learn about the particular
ailments of childhood.

But Dr West had the final words in
the meeting. He began by expressing his
pleasure at all the other contributions
that had been made. 'I rejoice, sir, that
the cause which I have to plead is so
good.' And he was optimistic that the
hospital on Great Ormond Street would
be the beginning of many more children's
hospitals. 'We may then hope that the
hospital which we are met together to
found today will not long continue to be
the only children's hospital in London.'

West's optimism was proven to be
well founded. By 1900 there were thirty
hospitals in Great Britain dedicated to the
care of children, eleven of which were
in London.

Who was 'Great Ormond?'

The 1st Duke of Ormonde had an eventful life at the court of Charles II. One of the most notable incidents saw him narrowly escape with his life on the evening of 6 December 1670, as he returned to his residence at Clarence House. He was ambushed by his arch-enemy, Colonel Blood, and four other assailants who tried to carry him off for the purpose of either ransom or murder.

Colonel Thomas Blood

Ormonde fought back, and escaped. Despite being fired at with pistols, Ormonde was not injured and in fact lived for another 18 years. He died in 1688, just a few years before Great Ormond Street was built.

Colonel Blood is chiefly famous for another event, however. Only a year after the failed plot on Ormonde, he tried to steal the crown jewels. He befriended the assistant keeper of the jewels at the Tower of London, then banged him on the head and bludgeoned the crown flat so he could fit it down his trousers! The attempt ended in failure, yet the King rather mysteriously decided to pardon him.

James Butler, Duke of Ormonde (1610–1688)

The hospital opens

The first home of The Hospital for Sick Children in the street named after Ormond was already familiar with medical practice. The well-proportioned Queen Anne townhouse at number 49 had once been the home of an eminent physician, Dr Richard Mead. Mead, who died almost a hundred years before the hospital was founded, was physician to many famous people including Queen Anne, George II and Isaac Newton.

On 14 February 1852, with no apparent ceremony, the porter opened the doors to what was now The Hospital for Sick Children. The large extension that Mead had built for his library became the first hospital ward. At this time there were just two physicians – West and Dr William Jenner – and ten beds. This number of beds would treble by the end of the hospital's first year.

The white stuccoed front of the original hospital building at 49 Great Ormond Street in a photograph from c.1870

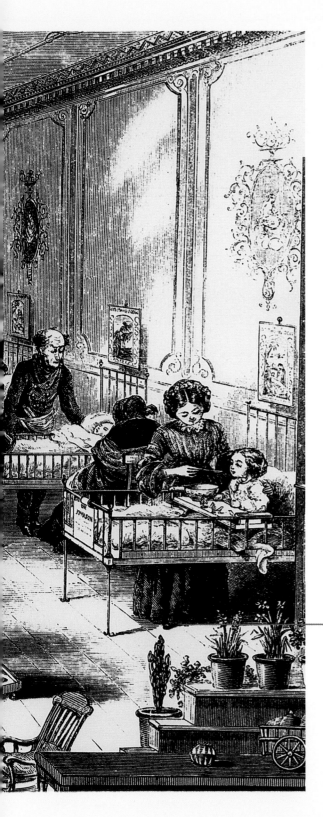

The stated aims of the hospital on opening were:

1. To provide for the reception and maintenance and medical treatment of the children of the poor during sickness and to furnish them with advice i.e. the mothers of those who cannot be admitted into the hospital.

2. To promote the advancement of medical science generally with reference to the diseases of children, and in particular to provide for the more efficient instruction of students in this department of medical knowledge.

3. To disseminate among all classes of the community, but chiefly among the poor, a better acquaintance with the management of infants and children during illness by employing it as a school for the education and training of women in the special duties of children's nursing.

William Jenner (far left) and Charles West (centre) are seen attending to patients in this drawing from 1856

The interior of the only ward in the new hospital was still decorated as a gentleman's 17th-century library when it first came into use

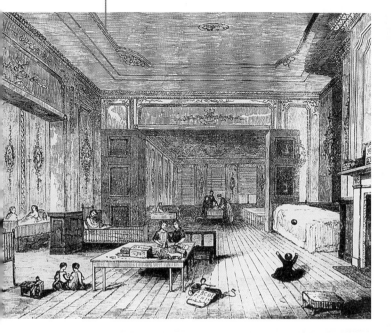

The first patient was three-and-a-half-year-old Eliza Armstrong. She had consumption, the non-medical word for phthisis (pulmonary tuberculosis), a common and often fatal disease of the time. She was admitted as an inpatient, though there was little that the hospital could really do for her apart from give her rest and good meals. She was sent home after three weeks, to attend as an outpatient. Like all patients at this time, Eliza came from a family that was too poor to pay for medical treatment.

Unlike today, there was no guaranteed treatment for those who could not afford it, and the hospital itself was funded by charitable donations rather than by the state. Financing the operation of the hospital was a constant challenge from the outset, and has remained so ever since. One of the methods was for wealthy 'subscribers' to recommend patients, but in the first few weeks fewer patients than expected actually attended.

'Drooping Buds'

It was at this point that Charles Dickens stepped in to promote the hospital. He wrote a piece called 'Drooping Buds' in his popular and widely respected periodical, *Household Words*, on 3 April 1852, just six weeks after the hospital had opened. His piece was not just an impassioned plea for widespread acceptance of the hospital for sick children, but a statement of its absolute necessity. 'More than a third of the whole population [of London] perishes in infancy and childhood,' he reported to his readers, 'the infant can only wail; the child is silenced by disease.' He made a compelling case for the need for a hospital to do something to

Dr West treats a sick child, whose mother stands weeping at the bed head. A nurse is also in attendance and in the background are some of the 'lady visitors' whose visiting continued almost unrestricted after that of parents had been curtailed to one afternoon a week

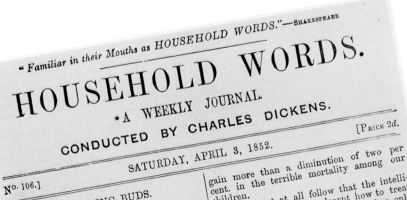

"Familiar in their Mouths as HOUSEHOLD WORDS."—SHAKESPEARE

HOUSEHOLD WORDS.

·A WEEKLY JOURNAL.

CONDUCTED BY CHARLES DICKENS.

[PRICE 2*d.*]

SATURDAY, APRIL 3, 1852.

Nº. 106.]

DROOPING BUDS.

IN Paris, Berlin; Turin, Frankfort, Brussels, and Munich ; in Hamburgh, St. Petersburgh, Moscow, Vienna, Prague, Pesth, Copenhagen, Stuttgard, Grätz, Brünn, Lemberg, and Constantinople ; there are hospitals for sick children. There was not one in all England until the other day.

No hospital for sick children ! Does the public know what is implied in this ? Those little graves two or three feet long, which are so plentiful in our churchyards and our cemeteries—to which, from home, in absence from the pleasures of society, the thoughts of many a young mother sadly wander—does the public know that we dig too many of them ? Of this great city of London—which, until a few weeks ago, contained no hospital wherein to treat and study the diseases of children—more than a third of the whole population perishes in infancy and childhood. Twenty-four in a hundred die, during the two first years of life ; and, during the next eight years, eleven die out of the remaining seventy-six.

Our children perish out of our homes : not because there is in them an inherent dangerous sickness (except in the few cases where they are born of parents who communicate to children heritable maladies), but because there is, in respect of their tender lives, a want of sanitary discipline and a want of medical knowledge. What should we say of a rose-tree in which one bud out of every three dropped to the soil dead ? We should not say that this was natural to roses ; neither is it natural to men and women that they should see the glaze of death upon so many of the bright eyes that come to laugh and love among them—or that they should kiss so many little lips grown cold and still. The vice is external. We fail to prevent disease ; and, in the case of children, to a much more lamentable extent than is well known, we fail to cure it.

Think of it again. Of all the coffins that are made in London, more than one in every three is made for a little child : a child that has not yet two figures to its age. Although science has advanced, although vaccination has been discovered and brought into general use, although medical knowledge is tenfold greater than it was fifty years ago, we still do not

gain more than a diminution of two per cent. in the terrible mortality among our children.

It does not at all follow that the intelligent physician who has learnt how to treat successfully the illnesses of adults, has only to modify his plans a little, to diminish the proportions of his doses, for the application of his knowledge to our little sons and daughters. Some of their diseases are peculiar to themselves ; other diseases, common to us all, take a form in children varying as much from their familiar form with us as a child varies from a man. Different as the ways are, or ought to be, by which we reach a fault in a child's mind, and reach a fault in the mind of an adult ; so, not less different, if we would act successfully, should be our action upon ailments of the flesh. There is another thing, also, which puzzles the physician who attends on children. He comes to us when we are ill, and questions us on our answers he is taught, in very many cases, to base a large part of his opinion. The infant can only wail ; the child is silenced by disease ; or, when it answers, wants experience, and answers incorrectly. Again, for life or death, all the changes in the sickness of a child are commonly very rapid : so rapid, that a child which suffers under an acute disease should be seen at least every five or six hours by its medical attendant. He knows how swiftly and how readily the balance may be turned upon which hang life and death. He may have been to Paris or to Vienna, and have studied in an hospital for children ; and, out of his experience, he may know how to restore the child whole to the mother's bosom. But all English students cannot go abroad for this good knowledge ; nor is it fit that they have need to do so. They have need at present. In a rough way, English practitioners of medicine no doubt administer relief to many children ; but, that they are compelled to see those perishing continually whom a better knowledge might have saved, none are more ready than themselves—the more skilful the more ready—to admit and to deplore.

The means of studying the diseases of children in London have been confined to one dispensary, and the general hospitals. In these,

Dickens's article Drooping Buds *was highly influential in the early fortunes of the hospital*

remedy the shocking mortality figures of children in London, and informed his audience that 'the want of a Child's Hospital is supplied. The Hospital for Sick Children, lately established and now open, is situated in Great Ormond Street, Queen Square'. It was not the last time that Dickens would prove of enormous service to the hospital, as will be seen.

Just a few weeks after the appearance of this article, and quite possibly as a direct consequence of it, Queen Victoria made a donation to the hospital and became its official patron. With royal endorsement, the hospital's name became emblazoned on the minds of the Victorian public. Great Ormond Street Hospital could now be confident of being able to move forward with its mission of treating 'the child first and always'.

Queen Victoria was the first monarch patron of the hospital. The tradition has continued ever since

31

Gary Lineker is a staunch supporter of Great Ormond Street Hospital and as patron of the Tick Tock Club is a regular visitor

I n 1991 my eldest son, George, was diagnosed with acute myeloid leukaemia. He was admitted to Great Ormond Street for treatment in November of that year.

When your child is ill you feel powerless, but the staff at the hospital were brilliant. We had a thousand questions we wanted to ask, and they answered all of them. It felt reassuring knowing more about George's disease; it lessened the

Gary Lineker, one of the country's most legendary footballers and presenter of 'Match of the Day', talks about his son George's time at Great Ormond Street.

fear. And I don't think we would have got through the illness were it not for the wonderful doctors and nurses.

George required months of chemotherapy – we spent that time basically living in the hospital. During our stay we got to know a number of other children with leukaemia and their parents.

Even after his successful treatment, George was not completely in the clear for another five years. We were, of course, massively relieved when we were told in 1998 that he had been cured, and hugely grateful to everyone who had helped to save his life. The biggest problem I have with my son now is the fact that he supports Manchester United!

I have been involved in fundraising for Great Ormond Street for many years, and I am very proud to be the patron of the Tick Tock Club, the central aim of which is to raise money for the construction of a world-class Heart and Lung Centre at the hospital. This will provide highly specialised care for seriously ill children and,

equally importantly, help to discover how to prevent heart disease from happening in the first place.

Great Ormond Street Hospital is a remarkable and humbling place – not just because of the treatments they provide for sick children such as my son, but because they use their expertise to develop new cures for conditions which, as yet, cannot be combated.

I am pleased to be able to help Great Ormond Street in its determination to remain one of the very best children's hospitals in the world.

Gary with some of the cardiac team at the hospital

Chapter 2

People

'In nursing an ounce of experience
is worth a pound of theory.'
Catherine Wood

The history of Great Ormond Street Hospital is as much a history of the many remarkable, pioneering and characterful people who have worked there and been involved with it, as it is one of an institution. This is a living history that carries on today, a procession of personalities that have joined together in caring for children at Great Ormond Street Hospital and who can be linked back, almost as though through a family tree, to the very beginnings of the hospital. There has always been passion and loyalty among people working at the hospital, and this is evident in so many accounts of people's working lives there since 1852. This passion comes from the recognition of how valuable that work is. It is the work of transforming children's lives for the better. This chapter tells the stories of some of the outstanding individuals who have helped the hospital to grow into the world-class centre it is today, and how staffing the hospital has changed dramatically since its early days.

An engraving of a nurse and child at The Hospital for Sick Children, from the front cover of the Christian Million magazine in 1884

Modest beginnings

The hospital now employs more than 2,500 people, but at the very beginning, when children's hospitals were a new and pioneering venture with unproven demand, there were only a handful of staff attending a single ward with ten beds, and a small outpatients department.

Dr Charles West and Dr William Jenner were the only two physicians to the hospital at its opening in 1852, together with a residential staff of a matron, house surgeon, dispenser, porter and nurses. The advertisement for the first matron, which appeared on 21 November 1851, stated that 'she must be a member of the Church of England, single and without encumbrances and between the ages of 30/45'.

The salary was £40 a year, including food and lodging. Mrs Willey was the successful candidate and she became Great Ormond Street Hospital's first matron. The other residential staff were also given salaries from the outset, except for the house surgeon who at first was expected to work voluntarily. After difficulties in recruiting for the post, however, it was decided in 1853 to award £20 a year to the post holder, given not as a salary but as 'expenses for rations'.

West and Jenner remained unpaid in their roles, as were all the senior medical staff at the hospital until the advent of the NHS in 1948. They earned their income from their entirely separate private practices, and saw hospital work as an opportunity to gain experience with a wide variety of cases, to enhance their reputation (thus hopefully improving their prospects in private practice), and as a form of social duty. In the one known photograph of Jenner, he looks a rather stern, if not ferocious, man and he was known, like West, for being a professionally uncompromising character. He was also renowned for being a workaholic, and when asked once what he did for amusement, he replied, 'Amusements! My amusement is pathological anatomy!'

Mrs Willey was made the first matron of the hospital in 1852

Sir William Jenner

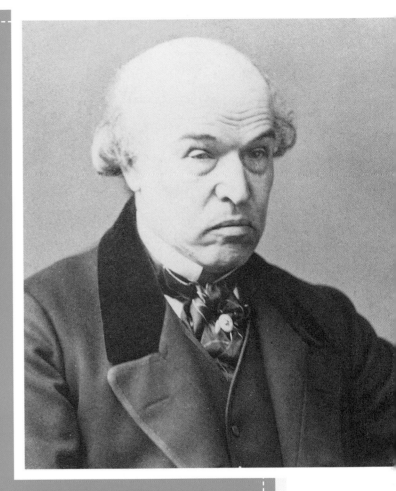

As with Charles West, children were said to adore Jenner, despite his rather severe appearance. One tale often told by Charles West was that of a patient at Great Ormond Street Hospital who said to Jenner, 'You are so like my daddy!' Jenner was naturally flattered, until he caught sight of the boy's father, who was, 'most villainously ill-looking'! He was, however, said to have taken the remark as a compliment, in the spirit it was evidently intended.

Jenner was very important in the early days of the hospital, for although West was responsible for much of the practicalities and organisation, Jenner had many important connections both within medicine and through his own prestigious private practice, which counted many famous names among its number. His influence was crucial in persuading critics that the hospital was a reputable venture.

Jenner had achieved eminence within his profession through a combination of ambition, hard work and steely determination. He made a name for himself when he published a monograph differentiating typhus and typhoid fevers in 1849, which had great consequences for public health. He ultimately became president of the Royal College of Physicians and remained so for six years.

In 1862 Jenner resigned from his post at Great Ormond Street Hospital to become Queen Victoria's Physician Extraordinary. Even then, he still checked the Queen's gifts of toys for the hospital to make sure they were safe for the children

He has been described by one author as the 'virtual dictator of his profession'.

Even after resigning his post at the hospital to become Queen Victoria's Physician Extraordinary in 1862, Jenner remained on the management committee and his 'friends in high places' were no doubt beneficial to Great Ormond Street Hospital's development.

The nurses

Both West and Jenner had the reputation of being extremely kind to their patients and popular with patients and parents alike. West realised, though, that it was the nurses at the hospital who had perhaps the most critical job to do. 'They are our best helpers,' he said, 'if indeed it be not rather true and I feel it is true, they are the real carriers-on of the hospital... They indeed are those who lead while we do but tread in their steps, and that often humbly and at a long distance.' Kind words indeed, but the reality was often that West's views reflected an overwhelming sense in which doctors regarded nurses merely as their handmaidens. In fact many of the patients benefited most from what the nurses were able to provide them with, namely clean clothes and bedding, good meals and warmth – all of which they would probably not have received at home. The major change in nursing at the time advocated that the nursing staff be managed by the matron, rather than the physicians, as until then the matron had only been responsible for housekeeping.

Reports on the quality of nursing at the time seem to suggest that changes were needed. One of the Great Ormond Street Hospital surgeons, Howard Marsh, later recollected that in 1861 'the nurse was a gossipy old Irish Gamp, called Money, who spent a great deal of her time on the staircase havering [gossiping] with the other nurses,' while a lady visitor, Louisa Twining, said of the nurses in 1860 that, 'what strikes me more than any actual misdemeanours or neglects, are the shortcomings in tone, motive and feeling, and the great want of unity and harmony between those who are engaged in this common work.' The 'Gamp' that Marsh refers to comes from the notorious midwife and night nurse Mrs Gamp in Dickens's *Martin Chuzzlewit* – 'Gamp is my name, and Gamp my nater'– whose common cry is 'Drink fair, wotever you do!'

Dr West described the Great Ormond Street Hospital nurses as 'the doers actually of the good work who shed a good influence on us as well as upon the children'

The superintendent

The rather negative stereotype of many nurses at the time led to an effort to improve standards, and a new post was appointed in 1862 – that of an unpaid lady superintendent. Isabella Babb, the daughter of a solicitor, was the first of these superintendents. Under her control, a new type of nurse entered the hospital – young, well-educated women who worked as sisters on a voluntary basis. These women usually had no experience of nursing, but their role was to supervise regular nurses and instil them with 'respectability and decorum'. The superintendent could have a great impact on the running of the hospital and, due to her unpaid position, could act quite independently from the medical staff, which did not please all of them.

The most famous of the superintendents was Catherine Wood, who was respected, but also feared, by many. She wrote a number of books, including a *Handbook of Nursing for the Home and Hospital* in which she wrote that 'in nursing an ounce of experience is worth a pound of theory'.

Isabella Babb was the first of the new lady superintendents who were brought in to the hospital to revolutionise nursing practice and also to instil poor children with middle-class values

Catherine Wood

Miss Wood had many traits that suggest she was the archetypal Victorian. Her beliefs in charity and moral duty were profound, and she worked without payment at the hospital for almost twenty-five years, between 1863 and 1888. She had a well-documented degree of strictness and severity about her, too.

Her discerning eye is revealed in her *Handbook of Nursing for the Home and Hospital*, in which she writes, 'The clever, bright attendant may succeed in hoodwinking the doctor. She has the sharpness to change her poultices just before the clinical rounds, to put on the clean linen for his visits; but the hot poultice and the clean sheets should be eyed with suspicion – they are the marks of a "gay deceiver".'

In 1863, aged twenty-two, Wood joined as one of the new breed of sisters under Isabella Babb, and in 1870 she became the matron of Great Ormond Street Hospital's newly opened convalescent home in Highgate, Cromwell House. She returned to Great Ormond Street Hospital in 1878, where she became lady superintendent for the next ten years. She was the most influential of all the lady superintendents at the hospital, laying the foundations for modern paediatric nursing and training.

There was a presentation given for Miss Wood to recognise her twenty-five years of service, which was reported in the *Nursing Record* in 1888: 'I am delighted to hear that Miss Wood last week attended at a meeting of the Governors of the Children's Hospital, GOS... and was presented by Lord Aberdare, the chairman, with a purse containing 100 guineas and a beautiful travelling clock.' The author comments that, 'one cannot help feeling that in any other country in Europe except our own, such work as Miss Wood has done would long ago have received more public and more substantial reward.'

Distinguished doctors

The hospital grew during the second half of the 19th century, first through the purchase of 48 Great Ormond Street in 1858, and then in 1875 with the opening of its first purpose-built hospital building. As the hospital grew, more people were needed to staff it, and more specialised roles were created. This was the era in which many of the eminent physicians and surgeons of the mid- to late Victorian period served at Great Ormond Street Hospital, often throughout their exceptional careers. These included Dr WB Cheadle, Dr WH Dickinson (an expert on kidney diseases) and Dr Samuel Gee.

Gee, who is most famous for describing coeliac disease, first worked at the hospital in 1862. The future poet laureate, Robert Bridges, who was best man at Gee's wedding in 1875, also worked briefly with him at Great Ormond Street Hospital. They had already worked together at Bart's, and it was there that Bridges wrote a Latin poem that featured Gee prominently. 'Had you not been my guide, philosopher and friend,' he writes of Gee, 'the learned school of medicine would be jeering at my headlong retreat.' One of Gee's colleagues tells a story of his sense of humour on the wards at the hospital. 'He once taught a small boy of five to tell visitors his complaint. Next day a lady asked the child, "Well, my little man, what have you got?" "Hydronephrosis, from the Greek words hudor, water, and nephros, the kidney," was the astounding reply.'

Sir Thomas Barlow was another distinguished Victorian who gave an astonishing seventy years' service to the hospital – a record that has never been surpassed. He also shares with Sir William Jenner the distinction of being appointed Physician Extraordinary to Queen Victoria. Just as Jenner was at Prince Albert's bedside when he died in 1861, so Barlow was with the Queen at her death in 1901.

Dr Samuel Gee

Barlow was in many respects a 'modern' man. He was in favour of women in medicine, against prescribing alcohol to children and, according to Poynton, 'nothing made him more upset than racial prejudice'

Sir Thomas Barlow

All those who attended the 1933 International Paediatric Congress in London had heard of Sir Thomas Barlow. He had started work at Great Ormond Street Hospital in 1875, and his paper on infantile scurvy from 1883 was especially famous. He was one of the eminent names of childhood medicine from the Victorian age. Very few of the delegates, who had come from all over the world, realised that Barlow was still alive. And when, at eighty-eight years old, Barlow stood up and invited the audience to thank the president of the congress, Sir Frederick Still, they had no idea who he was. But when Still enlightened the crowd, the 'entire congress applauded for five minutes without ceasing'. They were astonished to see that this legend was amongst them. Barlow remained an honorary consultant at Great Ormond Street Hospital until his death twelve years later, in 1945, at the age of ninety-nine.

Barlow was born in 1845 near Bolton, Lancashire, and he kept his Lancashire accent all his life. When he was sixteen, two members of his family, including a younger brother, died in a diphtheria epidemic. He studied in Manchester then came to London in 1866, where he studied medicine at University College alongside geology and palaeontology! On qualifying, he became house physician to Sir William Jenner at University College Hospital. Jenner was a great influence on him and helped his career enormously, particularly in recommending him to Queen Victoria.

He married one of the sisters at Great Ormond Street Hospital, Ada Helen Dalmahoy, in 1880 and they had three children. One child died in infancy and another died of trench foot in the First World War. Barlow was made a baronet in 1900.

Barlow's fame rested on his contributions to medical research. He made significant advancements in meningitis, rickets, rheumatism in children and Raynaud's disease, but his greatest achievement was to show, in 1883, that infantile scurvy was identical to adult scurvy, and that rickets was not an essential part of the disease. By 1894 this had come to be known as 'Barlow's Disease'.

He may have achieved his fame through scientific contributions, but Barlow's manner as a kind and gentle man, yet with very certain and generally liberal opinions, was what endeared him to his patients and peers alike. Many judged his success to lie in the feeling of confidence he inspired in his patients. A colleague from University College Hospital wrote that Barlow's 'kindly treatment of outpatients began to have a definite influence among us, till at last it was looked on as Bad Form to bark at the sick'!

Fine moustaches were evidently the fashion of 1894, as displayed in this picture of the medical staff that year. Dr Frederic Still, at the start of his eminent career, is seated on the ground at the front of the group

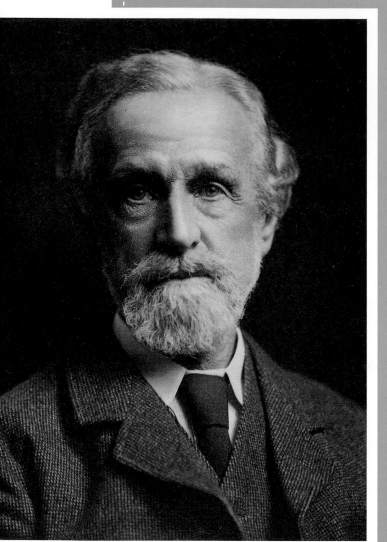

took the time to get to know the patient he was going to operate on.

Smith was one of the last of the hospital apprentices at Bart's, where he was instructed by the famous Sir James Paget, and he first came to Great Ormond Street Hospital in 1854 as a house surgeon. He resigned after a few months due to problems with his knee, but by 1861, after working in Paget's private practice, he was back again as assistant surgeon, and he remained at the hospital for the rest of his distinguished career until his retirement in 1898. He was Surgeon Extraordinary to Queen Victoria, and an excellent teacher of surgery, whose pupils were said to appreciate his wit and humour.

His work on cleft palate was at the forefront of surgical thinking at the time; indeed he remained open to innovation throughout his career, being one of the first surgeons in London to use Lister's antiseptic technique – though legend has it that he was not such a devotee that he stopped licking the end of the horsehair before threading the suture needle!

Sir Thomas Smith

Thomas Smith was not a surgeon who respected the textbook. He said of surgeons who wrote books that they were obviously the ones who never saw the interesting cases! He relied on his own observation and experience, rather than knowledge acquired from others. He also

It took a war to bring women into the hospital as doctors. This photograph from 1914 shows two female doctors – Miss Turner (left) and Miss Jukes (right)

Sir Thomas Smith, Great Ormond Street Hospital's first consulting surgeon, also had an appointment to the royal family as Surgeon Extraordinary. He and Barlow together were among those managing Edward VII's acute appendicitis in 1902 when they had to overcome the King's determination to defer the operation until after the coronation ceremony, a delay which would almost certainly have resulted in his death.

Another of Great Ormond Street Hospital's eminent surgeons of this period was Sir William Arbuthnot Lane, who served the hospital between 1883 and 1916. He was a consummate technician and an eccentric man, who became obsessed with constipation in adult patients (he wrote more than 100 papers on the subject) and dedicated much of his later life to efforts to improve public health, largely through diet. Although his contributions to surgery were both pioneering and remarkable for their variety (he

became world famous in at least four totally different fields), his legacy was somewhat more controversial than Smith's. It is said that 'his reputation suffered a little from poor imitation', but this is no doubt true of all surgeons who blaze a trail. It is also claimed that he was the inspiration for George Bernard Shaw's play *The Doctor's Dilemma*, a parody of doctors who are too willing to reach for the scalpel. Both parties denied the connection.

A lack of women

The medical staff in the 19th century at Great Ormond Street Hospital were all men. Jenner and West in particular were both adamant in their opposition to women entering the medical profession, though Sir Thomas Barlow had a more enlightened attitude. According to Barlow's grandson, Queen Victoria had held this very attitude against Barlow when Jenner

Sir William Arbuthnot Lane was a brilliant but controversial surgeon

recommended him to be her physician – she 'emphatically disapproved' of women doctors. Not until the First World War did women join the medical staff at Great Ormond Street Hospital, and after the war they were once again banished. Only in the late 1930s were women doctors finally allowed to practise in the hospital in peacetime – which was not to last for long.

The administration of the hospital, except in the office of the lady superintendent and matron, was similarly kept in male hands for many years. The first secretary was Mr HA Bathurst, who carried on his duties voluntarily for ten years before the post became salaried and he was taken over by Samuel Whitford. Whitford was the secretary between 1862 and 1885, when Adrian Hope took over. Hope, a frustrated *fin-de-siècle* dandy, was well-connected in London society and was a friend and neighbour of Oscar Wilde. He had a talent for fundraising and, it seems, for quarrelling with Catherine Wood, the formidable superintendent at the time. Sir Arthur Lucas was the chairman during Hope's tenure, a member of the board for forty-six years (1875–1921) and chairman for thirty (1891–1921), and it was his task to bang the heads of Hope and Wood together.

Adrian Hope

Hope was a tall and elegant man with a voguish sense of dress, a friend and neighbour of Oscar Wilde. He became the guardian of Wilde's children when he went to prison. His letters to his fiancée, Laura Troubridge, provide a fascinating private insight into life at Great Ormond Street Hospital from 1885, when Hope was appointed secretary. Despite his well-connected background, Hope was struggling to find enough money to marry his betrothed, and many of his letters record his deep frustration with financial matters. He met Catherine Wood on his first, somewhat reluctant visit to the hospital ('Goldsmid has induced me to apply' [to the post of secretary]) on 8 June 1885, when he said that 'everything was clean and airy'. Wood, however, was to become Hope's personal nemesis and they had many disputes in the three years they were at the hospital together (Wood resigned in 1888). These seemed often, at least on Hope's part, to consist of little more than juvenile point-scoring. On 15 June 1887, for example, Hope wrote: 'My committee is over and I have again beaten Miss Wood by getting my candidate for [the convalescent home in] Highgate against hers.'

Hope (rather ironically given his own chronic inability to raise funds for his marriage) had a particular talent for fundraising, due in large part to his good

Dr Poynton recorded his first impressions of Hope upon arriving at the hospital in 1900: 'The first Secretary I knew was Adrian Hope. It was said that at one time he was so ineffectual as to consider his dismissal, but in my day he was looked up to as remarkable.'

Hope died from complications arising from appendicitis in 1904, aged just forty-six, an event that Poynton remarks was a 'disaster and grief to all', for the man who had somewhat reluctantly joined the hospital had come to be enormously devoted to it.

connections. He was responsible for securing the speaking talents of Oscar Wilde for one of the anniversary dinners held annually for the hospital in February, for example. His close relationship with Wilde is clear in a letter Hope wrote: 'As I was walking home on Thursday I ran into the arms of Oscar Wilde who insisted on my dining with him, which I accordingly did and sat up talking with him in his vermilion garret until 2 of the clock.'

Adrian Hope, above and below. Dr Poynton said of Hope that he was 'tall and spare, he had an instinctive knowledge of how to meet people and organise affairs.' Nurse Ada Bois was the cartoonist who drew the portrait below with the caption 'We greatly enjoy watching on the distinguished visitors and Adrian Hope'

Sir Frederic Still

From a distance of a hundred years, Sir Frederic Still at the turn of the 20th century looks rather like JM Barrie, the author of *Peter Pan*. The two shared more than just a superficial physical similarity: both had siblings who died in childhood, both worked exceptionally hard to establish their careers from inauspicious backgrounds and both loved fly-fishing.

A lifelong bachelor Still, like Barrie, was utterly devoted to his mother but reserved in his other adult relationships. A biographer wrote that, 'In respect to his work he was punctilious, efficient, and an obsessive worker. Children loved him. An accurate and acute observer, he had

Donald Paterson persuades a doubtful Dr. Still that a B.P.A. must be founded.
[From a drawing by Mrs. Donald Paterson]

sound judgement and unrivalled experience and knowledge of children's diseases. During a career lasting over 50 years, Still's list of publications includes 108 papers and five books.' In 1906 he became Honorary Professor of the Diseases of Children at King's College, the first British chair in this new specialism.

Still is most famous for the disease that bears his name, which is a form of arthritis. He also did important work in many other fields, including congenital pyloric stenosis and congenital syphilis. With the encouragement of Donald Paterson, a Canadian paediatrician at Great Ormond Street Hospital, he helped to bring about the foundation of the British Paediatric Association in 1928 and was its first president.

In 1937 Still was appointed Physician Extraordinary to George VI and his family, and given a knighthood. He will be remembered as the first full-time paediatrician and the leading expert in childhood medicine during the early part of the 20th century.

(Above) Sir Frederic Still fishing
(Top right) Donald Paterson persuades Dr Frederic Still to help in founding the British Paediatric Association

Dr Frederick John Poynton, whose memoirs of his time at Great Ormond Street Hospital provide one of the most vivid accounts of the hospital during the early part of the 20th century

Edwardian doctors

The next generation of eminent doctors came to the fore at the turn of the century. Of these, Sir Frederic Still stands out as arguably the first doctor who devoted his entire career to caring for children alone. A biographer wrote that, 'As a pioneer of full-time paediatrics, as the first professor in this new discipline, and as inaugural president of the British Paediatric Association, Still has been called with justice the father of British paediatrics.'

Dr Frederick Poynton, by contrast, had captained Somerset in cricket, was a pioneer motorist and a keen singer. He was at the hospital from 1900 to 1934 and was president of the British Paediatric Association in 1931. He was said to be a great teacher, with 'humanity and spicy humour', and was personally most involved in the study of rheumatism, though he also took great interest in the general affairs of the hospital, working hard in the 1920s to secure an alternative site for it. He was heartbroken when the project failed.

Poynton had said that his colleague, Sir Archibald Garrod, 'represented all that was best in English medicine'. Garrod was also significantly ahead of his time in his research. A true pioneer in biochemistry, his 1908 book *Inborn Errors of Metabolism* was cited nearly forty years later by American Nobel Prize winners Beadle and Tatum, who wrote in tribute that, 'we had rediscovered what Garrod had seen so clearly many years before. By now we knew of his work and were aware that we had added little if anything new in principle.' Garrod's pioneering role in early genetics has been continued in groundbreaking work at Great Ormond Street Hospital, on treatments which have helped many children with genetic conditions.

Sir Archibald Garrod was an early pioneer of genetics and metabolic medicine

Support staff

As the hospital continued to expand, so demand increased for auxiliary professions such as technicians, pharmacists and radiographers. Mr CW Hale joined the staff in 1929 as a laboratory technician. He says that: 'laboratory technicians, especially junior ones, were regarded as a fairly low form of animal life. For example, we had to wear khaki brown laboratory coats so that there was no possibility of our being mistaken for doctors, who wore white coats. We looked like grocers! While I was there, the "seniors", Messrs Baker and Martin, were permitted to wear white coats with blue collars with the words 'Path Lab' in red on the lapels. They looked like milk roundsmen!'

A new generation

The famous names of medicine at Great Ormond Street Hospital in the 1920s and 30s included Frew, Cockayne, Thursfield and Moncrieff. Dr (later Sir) Alan Moncrieff was to become in 1946 the inaugural professor and chair of child health at the UCL Institute of Child Health, the research institute and postgraduate school that is linked to Great Ormond Street Hospital.

Sir Alan Moncrieff

Despite his excellent clinical career, Sir Alan Moncrieff will principally be remembered for being the first professor of child health at the UCL Institute of Child Health, the research and postgraduate centre connected with Great Ormond Street Hospital, in 1946. In 1964 Moncrieff told the story of how the formation of the UCL Institute of Child Health came about:

'Early in World War II it became apparent that the services for the care of sick children and the arrangements for the prevention of disease in childhood were not as good as they could be. Medical students had very little teaching on the subject of children's diseases and there was little organised post-graduate training available. Doctors in welfare clinics and the school health service had often never worked in a children's hospital or department. The turning point came in December 1941 when the Chief Medical Officer of the Ministry of Health addressed a meeting of children's doctors and firmly put the blame on them for the unsatisfactory state of affairs. The children's doctors accepted the challenge and the idea of 'Institutes of Child Health' was born'.

Moncrieff's appointment was seen as a wise one, partly because of his excellent career at Great Ormond Street Hospital before the war that had made him a respected figure. He had joined the staff at the hospital as house physician in 1925, aged just twenty-four. In 1934 he was appointed to the consulting staff.

He was a prolific writer with a clear and simple style, the medical correspondent for *The Times* and author and editor of many books.

The nursing staff at Great Ormond Street Hospital in 1921, with a four-legged friend

Sir Denis Browne

'Denis Browne was an extraordinary man, in whom strength of character and convictions stuck out like rugged and dangerous rocks upon which the wary might easily founder,' wrote one of Browne's colleagues in tribute after his death in 1967. This seems to have been a particularly apt description of Browne's character that was indomitable, rebellious and, for many, completely intimidating.

Browne was born in Melbourne, Australia, the son of an explorer, gold prospector and farmer, in 1892. He was sent to Europe while serving in the 13th Light Horse regiment in Gallipoli during the First World War, aged twenty-two. He was invalided home with typhoid, then spent the last two years of the war in France with Australian field ambulance units. He joined the hospital in 1922, and served the hospital in successive appointments as house surgeon, registrar, resident medical superintendent, consultant surgeon and finally emeritus surgeon. He was operating just two weeks before his death, aged seventy-four.

Browne was the founder of modern paediatric surgery in England, and he made a huge impact internationally. He made advances in many fields of surgery, particularly club feet, cleft palate and hypospadias. He pioneered surgery in the newborn and the development of paediatric surgery as a specialism in itself. He was also well known for inventing surgical instruments and other devices, such as splints and surgical boots, which were produced commercially and carried his name.

He was co-founder and first president of the British Association of Paediatric Surgeons, won numerous prestigious awards and accolades both in Britain and internationally, and was knighted in 1961.

A very tall man at 6 feet 5 inches, Browne was also, in his youth, a proficient tennis player. Legend has it that Browne would clear seats from the outpatients hall and practise his tennis shots there after hours, while his lodgings maid would constantly move his chair against the wall so that he could not do the same thing there. Browne grew so infuriated by this that he nailed his chair to the floor!

Browne was not only an excellent, world-leading surgeon, but also a designer of equipment such as splints for children's legs (below right)

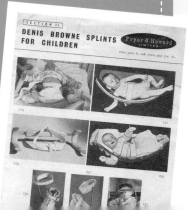

SECTION II

DENIS BROWNE SPLINTS FOR CHILDREN

Notable surgeons of the period included genito-urinary surgeon and author of the 100th anniversary book *Great Ormond Street 1852–1952*, Thomas Twistington-Higgins, pioneering all-rounder Sir Denis Browne and George Waugh, who specialised in ear, nose and throat surgery. Browne was a particularly eccentric but talented man, who was reputed to be the first full-time paediatric surgeon, and of whom there are a number of fantastic tales.

During the Second World War, Lord Southwood was chairman of Great Ormond Street Hospital, although in those years the hospital dealt with accidents and emergencies from the general population, rather than caring just for children. Southwood, who died in 1946, raised large sums of money for the hospital during the war years with a number of innovative appeals.

Specialism and excellence

In 1948 Great Ormond Street Hospital became part of the NHS. As the population of central London fell, the hospital's existing excellence in many clinical areas became even more specialised, so that more complex and multiple condition cases were referred from hospitals all over the country. This specialism and referral pattern continues to characterise Great Ormond Street Hospital today.

In this environment, the pace of change has been far more rapid than at any other time in the hospital's history, in terms of treatments, surgical techniques, drugs and technology, and many staff have been at the forefront of major medical advances. Some of the many leading

Mildred Creak at the opening of the Mildred Creak Unit

Mildred Creak

'Today we have reasonably unrestricted visiting, a flourishing school, a better appreciation of how to avoid harming the child's emotional life, and how to help parents in their distress, anxiety and sometimes guilt. This progress owes very much to Dr Creak's personality, skill and ever-ready help to her colleagues and to the nursing staff.'

This was Sir Alan Moncrieff's tribute to Mildred Creak on her retirement in 1964. The fact that this could also describe the situation in the 21st century shows what a seminal impact Creak had on Great Ormond Street Hospital. Since the early days of the hospital, visits from parents had been highly restricted because of concerns over infection. Both Creak and Moncrieff were very concerned about the impact this had on the psychological state of their patients, so increased the visiting hours for parents.

From 1942, when she started working at the hospital, Creak championed collaboration between paediatricians and psychiatrists, and withstood much initial scepticism from her colleagues in setting up the department for psychological medicine. Her work, and that of her department, was recognised when a unit at the hospital was named after her. Creak was exceptionally enthusiastic and hard working, and it is said that that when she retired from Great Ormond Street Hospital two men working full time had to be appointed to do her part-time job!

lights include Mildred Creak, the first female consultant at Great Ormond Street Hospital and a founder of child psychiatry in Britain, who established the psychological medicine department at the hospital; David Waterston and cardiologist Dr Richard Bonham-Carter, who made rapid advances in cardiac surgery; and David Matthews, who led major progress in plastic surgery. Sir Denis Browne continued to work at the hospital into the 1960s, an

David Matthews

'Two-hand Matthews' may sound like a gunslinger's nickname, but David Matthews earned this affectionate soubriquet for his ambidextrous skill as a plastic surgeon. He came to Great Ormond Street Hospital in 1947 and stayed for almost thirty years, retiring in 1976 at the very top of his field.

Matthews' prime clinical interests were in the management of cleft lip and palate, and of craniofacial abnormalities. But as well as his clinical excellence he also had a remarkable track record in promoting plastic surgery and working as an expert adviser in his field. He was highly involved in the advancement of plastic surgery internationally, and was instrumental in the formation of the International Confederation for Plastic and Reconstructive Surgery, serving as its first general secretary. He was also honorary member of the plastic surgical societies of fourteen countries, civilian consultant in plastic surgery to the Royal Navy, consultant adviser in plastic surgery to the Department of Health, and twice president of the British Association of Plastic Surgeons.

Matthews had a profound sense of duty and remained an active member of his local volunteer driver service well into his eighties, ferrying people to and from hospital who were often many years younger than himself. He died in 1997, aged eighty-six

Audrey Callaghan

Lady Audrey Callaghan presided over an unsettled period of the hospital's history, and was in the potentially difficult situation in the late 1970s, and particularly during the 'winter of discontent' of 1978–79, of having a husband who was prime minister. Despite this she was always modest and unassuming, even travelling from Downing Street to Great Ormond Street Hospital by bus.

The Times recorded at Lady Callaghan's death in 2005 that, 'it will probably be her long years of service as the chairman of the board of governors of the world-renowned Great Ormond Street Hospital for Sick Children from 1969 until 1982, followed by her chairmanship of the special trustees from 1984 to 1990 and as an appeal trustee from 1984 onwards, that will be regarded as her major contribution to the development of progressive services for children.' She also remained on the board at the UCL Institute of Child Health until 1995, and made many other contributions to children's welfare beyond Great Ormond Street Hospital.

After her chairmanship ended, she was instrumental in bringing about the so-called 'Callaghan amendment' to the Copyrights Act of 1988, which allowed Great Ormond Street Hospital to continue to receive royalties from *Peter Pan*. In recognition of her role, Lady Callaghan's name is inscribed alongside that of JM Barrie's on the Peter Pan statue near the entrance to the hospital.

Lady Audrey Callaghan lends a hand with the construction of the hospital's cardiac wing

acknowledged leader in his field. The most recent pioneering work of the hospital is looked at in the chapters on medical advances and the future of Great Ormond Street Hospital.

The people of the future

The administration of the hospital has grown in complexity, partly because of its increased size and partly because of the immense complexity of the NHS. Although often seeming rather anonymous figures, chairmen, trustees, directors, managers and administrators remain absolutely vital to the smooth running of the organisation, and there are many who have dedicated their lives to Great Ormond Street Hospital just as the medical professions have. Lady Callaghan was one such figure. She devoted twenty-six years, between 1969 and 1995, to work at Great Ormond Street Hospital and the UCL Institute of Child Health.

The varied kaleidoscope of personalities who have worked at Great Ormond Street Hospital and the sheer volume of characters, their achievements, pioneering work and humorous stories are bewildering to attempt to chronicle. This account is very much the edge of a vast

spectrum – many thousands of people throughout the history of the hospital have played a part in its successful operation. The great champions of Great Ormond Street Hospital now, though, are those who are working at the hospital in treating the sick children of today, and providing innovation, new facilities and improvements for the treatment of sick children in the future.

Chapter 3

Children

'If men do not keep on speaking terms with children, they cease to be men, and become merely machines for eating and earning money.'
John Updike

There are many separate parts to Great Ormond Street Hospital – its buildings, its staff and its technology to name just a few – but there is one part that is essential for all the others to exist: the patients. The children define the mission of the hospital, and Great Ormond Street Hospital has no meaning and no purpose without the children in its care. Beyond this, however, the patients are also the heartbeat and the voice of the place; they give life to the buildings, motivation and dedication to the staff and meaning to the technology. This is not sentimentalism; it is a statement of fact. And so it has always been, even when in the early days the building was a 17th-century townhouse, the staff numbered just a handful and the technology and treatments were extremely primitive.

Patients play with a sundial at Tadworth Court, which was a country base for Great Ormond Street Hospital from 1927 to 1982

For many years, a register was kept of all children admitted under the age of two. These are some of the entries from 1875

Primitive treatments

When Great Ormond Street Hospital opened, the lack of medical knowledge meant that patients received very little of what by modern standards we would call medical treatment. As many of the patients came from impoverished homes, they benefited merely from the fulfilment of basic human needs that had been denied to them, such as healthy, regular meals, cleanliness and warmth. There were no sophisticated drugs, and surgery was limited to procedures such as the lancing of abscesses, amputation of limbs and removal of bladder stones. Chloroform, which with ether was the principal anaesthetic of surgery in the Victorian era, had only been in use since 1847 and it was still not widely used when Great Ormond Street Hospital opened. Mortality rates from surgery were very high, due mainly to poorly understood post-operative infection. Surgery was therefore generally avoided wherever possible.

Age limits

The initial rules stated that only patients between two and ten years old could be admitted. Older children were expected to go to adult hospitals, while the younger ones, it was felt, should not be separated from their mothers. Dr Charles West had other ideas, however, and in December 1852 he explained to the hospital secretary that there happened to be two babies in the hospital at the time: one, he said, would have died if it had not been admitted, and the other, although not at risk of death, could not be given proper attention at

A photograph of a patient on Victoria ward, taken just a few years after the opening of the hospital's first purpose-built building in 1875

1875			1875	
Date	Name of Child	Age	Reason for Admission	Medical Officer
Feb. 23rd	William Walls	1yr 2 mos.	Requiring an operation, which could only be performed on an in-patient for double harelip. To be discharged in a few days — .	Mr Smith.
Feb. 23rd	Luckhurst Wm	1yr 8 mos.	Large spleen — purpura — in a dangerous condition	Dr Gee
Feb. 26	Williamson Florence	1yr 11 mos.	Syphilitic disease of the epiphyses of both femora & both tibia requires great care & attention to save the legs.	Mr Smith
March 1st	J. Chamberlain (Boy) (has since died. (clear. 4th)	1yr 6 mos.	Pulmonary Catarrh, with scattered solidifications in the lungs. requires great care —	Dr Gee

home due to lack of space. The number of infants admitted gradually increased over the years, from thirty-two in 1862 to fifty-four in 1876 and eighty in 1881. Over time, due to the persistence of the medical staff, it became accepted practice for the hospital to care for these infants, even though, strictly speaking, it remained against the organisation's rules until the 20th century.

The upper age limit was soon moved to twelve years old, where it remained until after the Second World War. In the 1950s, individual departments began to treat older patients before this was written into the hospital rules. This was the beginning of 'adolescent medicine', which ultimately saw patients up to the age of nineteen being treated at the hospital.

The first patients

The first inpatient at Great Ormond Street Hospital was three-and-a-half-year-old Eliza Armstrong, who was suffering from pulmonary tuberculosis. The first outpatient, George Parr, was two years old and was suffering from catarrh and diarrhoea.

There was some suspicion of the hospital at first, and West realised there was work to be done to convince the parents of sick children that a hospital ward was the best place for their offspring. 'At first,' he said, 'it seemed almost as

The Mary West Cot was named after the first wife of the hospital's founder, Dr Charles West

The clinical case note for Thomas Peam, who lived on Hackney Road. On 2 May, 1852, just one month after admission, Thomas died from tuberculosis. He was five years old

14,500 a year by 1880, and continued to rise into the 20th century. It seemed as though the hospital had succeeded in its work of spreading its reputation.

Visiting

The large wards in the 1875 building (known as 'the hospital in the garden') were warmed by open fires in the centre and had polished wooden floors. The beds were set out in long rows. Dr Poynton recalled standing in front of the central fire on Annie Zunz ward, 'and in the winter months the fire repeatedly smoked, or it was stoked up so fiercely that I accused sister of attempting to dry up my cerebro-spinal fluid!'

Parental visiting was initially encouraged. Parents were allowed to see their children four days a week, and were encouraged to help the

if a Children's Hospital were not needed, for so few were the applicants... The Hospital had its character to make among the poor.' After a few uncertain months, however, the number of patients increased steadily through the 19th century, as the hospital itself grew in size – first with the purchase of the neighbouring house, number 48, in 1858, and then with the opening of the first purpose-built building in 1875. The pattern of this growth was already evident in the hospital's second year, when the number of inpatients admitted increased from 143 to 190, and the outpatients from 1,250 to 4,251. This also shows that the vast majority of patients were seen as outpatients. This remains the case today, as staff believe it is better for children to be kept out of the hospital if at all possible. The number of outpatients had risen to more than

After 1854, visitor rules became increasingly strict. This notice from 1886 bans all children from visiting their brothers, sisters and friends

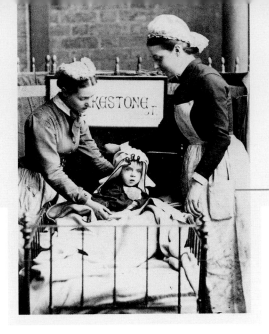

Tucking up a patient in the 'Folkestone Cot'. The cot was named after the Viscountess Folkestone in 1880

children but also to be increasingly involved with the whole treatment process. This remains so today. Modern facilities for parents at the hospital provide accommodation for at least one parent for every night of their child's stay.

A strange treatment

nurses, particularly with washing the clothes and bedding! But in 1854 the medical staff recommended to the management committee that parental visiting be reduced to two days a week, as they believed that recent outbreaks of measles and scarlet fever had been introduced by visitors to the hospital. Although parental visits were restricted, there were no such restrictions on the 'lady visitors' who were an important source of charity to the hospital. There were many more outbreaks of highly contagious childhood fevers throughout the 19th century, and the visiting hours were progressively diminished until they were restricted to an hour and a half on Sunday afternoons. This remained the case until the 1950s, when the psychological needs of the children at the hospital began to be more seriously addressed, and it was realised that such a restrictive regime was potentially harmful to them. From then on, parents began not only to visit their

Restrictions on visiting are not the only aspect of the patient experience from the 19th century that seem surprising today. The fact that patients were prescribed alcohol seems remarkable – shocking, even – in the 21st century, although it was widespread in hospitals at the time. During a period of seven weeks from September to November in 1857 the hospital purchased 29 bottles of port, 17 of white wine, four of brandy and 191 pints of porter (a type of dark beer). The wine and

Alcohol was widely prescribed in the 19th century, as this register from 1881 shows

Janine Goulding's story

Janine was born in the bedroom of her parents' house in Preston, Lancashire, in 1957, and it was immediately clear that she was not an entirely normal baby. She was born with a number of congenital (inherited) abnormalities, including a double bladder, where one part was inside her body and one part outside, and dislocation of both her hips. Initially it was thought she would not survive, but after a few days she was referred to Great Ormond Street Hospital. Janine was an inpatient and an outpatient at the hospital until 1972.

Janine has many clear memories of her time at the hospital. 'We had to travel by train from Preston. Euston Station seemed huge, and for many years I dreamed the same dream about getting separated from my mum and being lost... I was placed under the care of Professor Andrew Wilkinson, of whom I have fond and precious memories. He was a huge giant of a man in every way, and had the most gentle and reassuring smile and eyes I have ever seen... I felt very safe in his care. The feeling of safety came partly from the fact that these people seemed to understand me and not express shock and bewilderment, which is often what I experienced with the medical profession and teachers at home; unlike Great Ormond Street Hospital who were used to caring for people like me.'

Most of Janine's major surgery was performed in the first five years of her life, but her care continued until she was fifteen, when she had her last major operation. Remembering the surgery, she recalls that, 'everybody peering down at me seemed like giants, then the facemask would be pulled down and a friendly reassuring smile and voice from the anaesthetists.'

Her treatment was successful and Janine enjoyed a normal life. She married in 1979, had two daughters and a career in nursing, and more recently became a delighted grandmother. She says that this was possible not just because of the medical treatment she

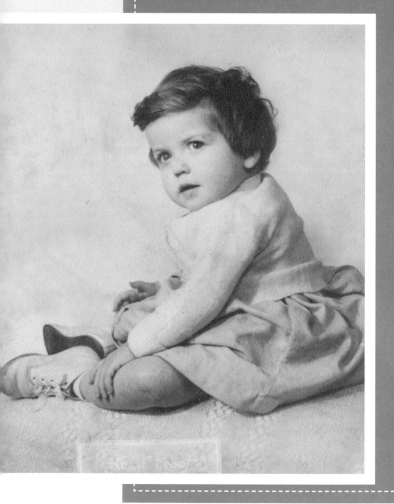

received at Great Ormond Street Hospital, but also because of the emotional care she found there. She remembers in particular one registrar, Dr Caroline Doig. 'One day she spent ages just going through all that was wrong with me, explaining all the different aspects and consequences of my condition. She talked openly and in a helpful way about my sexual development, marriage and having babies, things I couldn't ask my mum about.'

Far left: Janine Goulding, aged eighteen months. Above: Janine in 2006, third from right, with her husband, two daughters, son-in-law and grandchildren

'Great Ormond Street Hospital treated me and my family as whole people, not just another patient and her family; and when my mum fought to get me into mainstream education, they fought with us. And we won.'

brandy were for the children; the porter for the resident medical staff. The fact that there were only thirty beds in the hospital at the time suggests a prodigious consumption of alcohol by the patients! One of the most eminent physicians at Great Ormond Street Hospital, Sir Thomas Barlow, campaigned vociferously against this practice, but his views were not widely accepted and the tradition continued into the early years of the 20th century.

A healthy diet

On a more wholesome note, Dr Hillier's dietary recommendations from 1867 suggest that the patients' care was being looked at not only in terms of surgery and treatments, but in terms of the 'whole child'. He proposed that:

1. Roast beef be given for dinner one day a week
2. Convalescents be given pudding three days a week
3. Green vegetables be provided one day a week, except when very expensive
4. A slice of bread and butter be given for supper when desired.

Patients play in the gardens of Cromwell House soon after it opened in 1869

At the time the diet was a good one, certainly compared to what most of the children received at home.

Convalescence

From 1869, patients were cared for not only at the central London site, but also in a convalescent home in more tranquil surroundings, first at Cromwell House in Highgate, which was then still outside the turmoil of the city, and from 1927 at Tadworth Court in Surrey.

A boy recorded only as 'Willie Curtin' was admitted in about 1870 with chronic hip disease and other complications. He stayed at Great Ormond Street Hospital before being sent to recuperate at Cromwell House and then Margate, where the hospital kept a couple of beds reserved for long-term convalescent patients to enjoy the Victorian panacea of 'sea air'. On his return to London, the boy was asked whether he liked the seaside. 'It was lonely there,' he is said

Willie Curtin

Children in the garden of Great Ormond Street Hospital at the beginning of the 20th century

69

to have replied, 'You takes a long time to get used to a place, and there ain't no place like this hospital!'

Technology brings change

Electricity was first used to light the operating theatre at the main Great Ormond Street Hospital site in 1898, and in the following years it replaced the gas lamps throughout the hospital. In the early 20th century, as technology and innovation gathered momentum, many other aspects of the patient experience changed rapidly. Surgery benefited from improved anaesthetics and drugs to control infection. The 'electricity department' – the forerunner of the radiology (X-ray, CT and MRI) department – began to offer 'electrical therapy' and 'sun-ray treatment', while other new facilities, such as the pathology laboratory, enabled more accurate and earlier diagnoses.

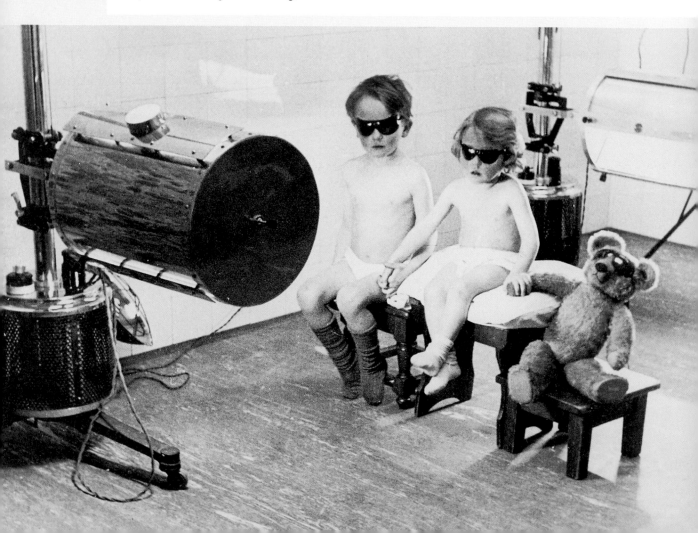

Christmas has always been a special time for children at the hospital. This is Christmas on Helena ward in about 1910

Patients from far and wide

There was also a change in the patients who were coming to Great Ormond Street Hospital. The hospital had established itself with a number of industrious doctors and surgeons as an international centre of excellence in the teaching and research of childhood disease. Its reputation attracted more patients from outside the immediate vicinity of the hospital, including from all over Britain and beyond. It is a trend which continues to this day, with approximately half of Great Ormond Street Hospital's patients currently coming from outside London, referred to the hospital because it is one of the few specialising in many different complex and rare conditions.

Margaret Smith first went to the hospital in 1932. 'My memory of it was that it was an old building, even then, and I was small, it's true, but the windows were high. I can remember the big

old-fashioned radiators – lumpy old radiators. But I remember that it was kind, everything was for you and you got that feeling even as a tiny child.'

In 1935, the first known surviving quadruplets in Britain, the 'St Neots' quads', were born in their family home in Cambridgeshire. The hospital sent four nurses from their private nursing service to look after them, and a spokesperson said that 'the hospital is meeting the cost of these nurses going down for we realise that the parents are poor people... We are glad to give this help because the quadruplets are a unique case'. There was enormous press interest and a clamour for pictures of the babies. All four survived, and have lived long and relatively normal lives away from the public eye.

Children undergo 'sun-ray treatment' at the hospital in 1922. Until 1930 the treatment was largely used to treat rickets, lupus and tuberculosis

The St Neots quads

Jamie Kenningham

As a child Jamie never thought he would make it to adulthood. 'I was always told, and my parents were told, that I would probably get to my early teens and I would have had a very good innings, really.' But not only did Jamie survive, he is living a full, happy and successful life. In a remarkable twist to an extraordinary tale, in October 2006, aged twenty-six, Jamie joined the Great Ormond Street Hospital Charity as a manager in the major gifts fundraising team.

Jamie was born in 1980 with multiple congenital heart defects, and he was operated on the same evening at Hammersmith Hospital to save his life. The main diagnosis was of pulmonary atresia, which means that the pulmonary valve in his heart was missing. This also gave Jamie a blue (cyanotic) appearance because the blood circulating through his body was not fully oxygenated. He came to be known as 'the blue baby', and was photographed by David Bailey as part of the Wishing Well appeal at Great Ormond Street Hospital in 1987.

From Hammersmith Jamie was transferred to Great Ormond Street Hospital, where he underwent open heart surgery in 1981. Over the following ten years he had open heart surgery on four more occasions, and further surgery to mend scar tissue resulting from the previous interventions. Of his childhood Jamie remembers, 'I did have a strange childhood; I missed a lot of school and I was quite poorly, really... One of the best things for me was meeting other children who had similar problems to me; it made me realise that I wasn't a freak.'

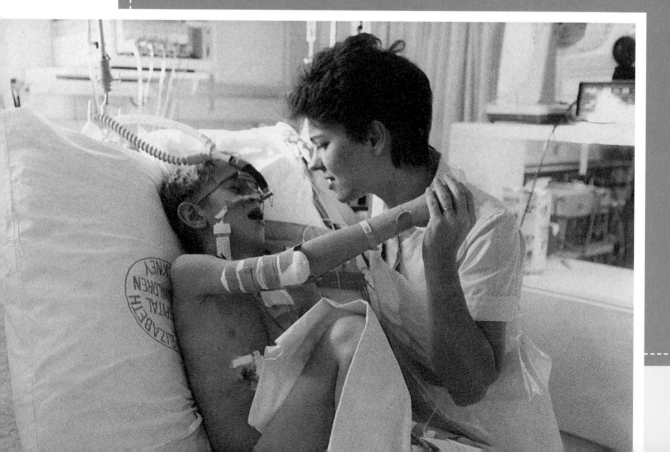

In Jamie's work fundraising for the hospital charity, he often takes potential donors on tours around the hospital. On his first such visit back to the cardiac ward where he had been a patient, he was able to reassure a child who had undergone a similar procedure to his own. 'We met this kid who was a spitting image of me when I was a child; he'd had the same surgery and the same scar. His mum was there and I explained to them what we were doing and then I said, "I've got the same scars as you" and told them about my life. We were talking for around twenty minutes; a crowd gathered... people could not believe my story.'

Jamie's health started to improve significantly as he entered his teens, though he still suffered at times from an irregular heart beat (arrhythmia). But this also improved considerably by the time he was fourteen, so he enjoyed a relatively normal life for much of his teenage years. As an adult Jamie's pulmonary valve had to be replaced again, as implants only have a limited life span. This time, however, he was able to avoid the invasive procedures that had been used during his childhood, because of an innovative new technique pioneered by a cardiac surgeon at Great Ormond Street Hospital, Professor Philipp Bonhoeffer. Rather than opening up the chest cavity, which would have held significant risk for Jamie due to the

Left: Over a ten-year period, Jamie had open heart surgery four times. Of his time in Great Ormond Street Hospital he says, 'I have some quite shocking memories – intensive care, tubes everwhere and lots of pain – but equally I also have some quite fond memories.'
Above right: Jamie in 2007

number of times he had been operated on already, the Bonhoeffer technique allows for a valve to be inserted into the heart via a small opening in the neck. After the treatment in June 2005 Jamie was back at home after two days, rather than the two months that was the norm during his childhood. To date, more than 155 children and adults have been treated successfully using this procedure.

By 2006 Jamie had had seven years' experience in fundraising for a number of charities, before he applied for the job of development manager at Great Ormond Street Hospital Children's Charity.

Jamie tries to get large donations to support the work of the hospital. On some of the visits to potential donors, he is accompanied by cardiac surgeon Professor Martin Elliot, who operated on Jamie three times. 'That's unusual, I guess,' says Jamie, 'but I'm glad I can help in whatever way I can to raise money for essential steps forward at the hospital, such as the new Heart and Lung Centre.'

A nurse and child at the start of the Second World War

Second World War

The only time when the hospital was virtually 'childless' was during the Second World War. The patients were sent to Tadworth Court and other places outside central London, while the hospital treated accident and emergency cases as a 'casualty clearing station'. The children gradually returned towards the end of the war.

One boy who was in Great Ormond Street Hospital for an operation when the war ended remembered the nurses taking turns to join in the victory celebrations outside, and coming back with flags for the children. His most vivid memory was of the house surgeons bursting into the ward, laughing and covered in dust, having just knocked down the brick blast wall which had provided protection from exploding bombs for nearly six years.

A holistic approach

Patients since the end of the Second World War have benefited from numerous advances at Great Ormond Street Hospital, and in paediatric medicine in general, in terms of better drugs, massive improvements in surgery and other treatments, but also because of a more modern sense of holistic care. This has led to such

Hospital toys have always played an important part in the children's road to recovery

Children pick grapes in the gardens of Tadworth Court, the main refuge for Great Ormond Street Hospital patients during the Second World War

improvements as the introduction of a proper hospital school, and the increasingly important role of play specialists who provide support and development through a variety of activities. These can be vital to the children's mental and physical progress. Play has always been important at Great Ormond Street Hospital, as can be seen from the toys that are so evident in early pictures of the hospital, and from the fact that Queen Victoria herself donated toys at Christmas.

Treatment for all

In more recent times, the length of stay of inpatients has been greatly reduced, and the number of day cases (children who have minor surgery in a single day and do not require admission) has increased. This means that the children can spend far more time in familiar surroundings which, in all but a very few cases, is better than staying on a hospital ward. In 2006

Afternoon tea on the ward in 1939

half of Great Ormond Street Hospital's patients were from London, and more than a third were from non-white ethnic groups. The hospital now provides better care for children than at any other time in its history, in terms of the types of treatment, the latest technologies and, since the Second World War, an increasing emphasis on holistic care and the creation of a therapeutic environment in which clinical results are just one part of the care of children and their families.

Future generations

The current situation of the hospital is by no means ideal in a number of respects, however. The need remains to provide the best possible environments for both inpatients and outpatients, with improved buildings equipped with better facilities for both staff and patients. To maintain Great Ormond Street Hospital's standing as a truly world-class children's hospital requires significant funding that cannot be provided solely from the government. The scepticism of parents in the first few months of the hospital in 1852 should not be forgotten. It was felt then that the best place for children to be cared for was at home. This is surely right; the hospital may strive to be as child-friendly as possible, but it is essentially a last resort for sick children who cannot be helped elsewhere. The hospital therefore continues to work towards limiting the time children have to spend there, however well designed it may be.

Perhaps this is one instance of the past being instructive. The dire living conditions of many in 1852 may seem remote today, but social conditions, particularly poverty, are still important factors in the development of some childhood diseases. In this respect 'the child first and always' is a motto which should arguably be foremost not only at the hospital, but in society as a whole. Discussion about and action on children's welfare has historically often been rooted in sentimentality, which looks more at the symptoms of problems than their causes. Great Ormond Street Hospital has a continuing role to play in the process of looking beyond sentimentality by not only treating sickness, but also promoting good health and the conditions required for it.

Simeon Lynch-Prime

'I think I cried every day,' says Simeon's mother, June, of the time when Simeon was being treated for a malignant brain tumour at Great Ormond Street Hospital. 'My partner was much calmer, but I got myself in a state and when Simeon saw me crying I would tell him that it was hay fever.'

Initially, June thought it was strange that Simeon's speech had not developed as early as either of his two elder siblings, Kedeem and Makeda, but it was only when he started to have problems with his balance, as he was turning two years old, that she began to worry. At first, tests at their GP surgery did not pick up any abnormality, but the balance problem worsened and Simeon had cuts and bruises from falling over so often. 'I knew then that something was wrong,' says June. A reflex test and then a scan at their local hospital, the North Middlesex Hospital, confirmed her worst fears – Simeon had a brain tumour that required urgent attention.

Great Ormond Street Hospital is the largest treatment centre for children with cancer in the UK, and the third largest in the developed world. It treats one-fifth – approximately 65–75 patients a year – of all children in the UK with brain tumours, specialising in very young children.

Five days after Simeon's scan in the summer of 2005, the tumour was removed at Great Ormond Street Hospital by neurosurgeon Professor Richard Hayward. Unfortunately, two days after the operation Simeon got an infection and spent eleven days in intensive care. The whole family stayed at the patient hotel nearby and spent time with Simeon, 'willing him to get better'. He pulled through, but he was very weak – too weak for the chemotherapy he needed to ensure the malignancy had been removed completely.

Simeon gradually recovered, and June recalls how one day the consultant in charge of Simeon's care, Professor Hayward, asked her if she had seen her son yet. At that moment Simeon pedalled past her on a tricycle, looking extremely happy! He was now strong enough to start the chemotherapy, though this was another difficult time for Simeon and his family. 'If Sim was good then so was I,' says June. 'If he handled his chemo well then we were happy, but if he was sick with it then I was very upset.' She remembers brushing the hair of her three-year-old son, and all of it coming out, which she found particularly distressing. But Simeon made it through the chemotherapy and subsequent radiotherapy. Scans gave him the all clear, and he started at his local primary school in October 2006. In March 2007 Simeon celebrated his 5th birthday with a disco party, his hair almost completely grown back. He wears a hearing aid and glasses, and requires speech therapy and a support worker at school, but June says that 'he is absolutely brilliant and more than

holds his own with the other kids'.

Despite the family's traumatic experience, June says that Simeon 'absolutely loved his time at Great Ormond Street Hospital. He loved the play specialists, and when he was having his treatment he would lie back and

Simeon dresses up as Peter Pan in Kensington Gardens with the author of Peter Pan in Scarlet, *Geraldine McCaughrean*

stick his thumb up in the air to say that he was okay – as far as he was concerned it was his hospital.'

GMTV presenter Fiona Phillips talks about her son's treatment at Great Ormond Street.

My little boy, Mackenzie, came to Great Ormond Street Hospital in 2003 suffering from severe chronic eczema. It was a great relief to me to know that his condition was finally being dealt with properly, after months of sleepless nights and blood-stained sheets, and trying just about everything and everyone to try to help him.

I remember, after our first visit to the outpatients department, going home and laying Mackenzie on the bed knowing that finally he was going to get the best possible treatment. It was like a miracle, to be honest – literally an overnight cure after all the pain he had endured, and all the heartache and worry my husband and I had gone through.

The whole team in dermatology was brilliant. They fully explained the procedure for home treatment, so that we left full of confidence as to what would happen next.

I think that Great Ormond Street Hospital is the gold standard – well, platinum, actually. When one thinks of sick children being transformed through professionalism and loving care into healthy, prospering kids, one name comes to mind, and that is Great Ormond Street Hospital.

Since Mackenzie's treatment I have attended a number of events at the hospital, including opening the new bone marrow transplant laboratories in September 2003.

I want to say a big 'thank you' to everybody at the hospital who helped to cure my son.

Fiona opening the bone marrow transplant laboratories in 2003 with patient Kristina Cartwright-Riley and her sister, Rebecca

Chapter 4

Breakthroughs

*'Man masters nature not by force, but by understanding.
This is why science has succeeded where magic has failed.'*
Jacob Bronowski

The big news in modern medicine has always been about major steps forward in the understanding of disease and how to treat it; seminal developments such as Louis Pasteur's work on bacteria and vaccination and Alexander Fleming's on penicillin continue to appeal to the popular imagination today. Great Ormond Street Hospital has a strong heritage of being at the forefront of new developments in understanding childhood disease and treating sick children. These developments have also often succeeded in capturing the popular imagination, as witnessed by countless newspaper headlines and articles in professional journals. By virtue of the fact that it was the first children's hospital in the English-speaking world, Great Ormond Street Hospital immediately defined itself as pioneering, and throughout its history it has remained consistently groundbreaking and innovative.

The pharmacy at Great Ormond Street Hospital in the 1930s. Major advances in pharmaceuticals have played an enormous role in improving the treatments available to children at the hospital. There has also been significant progress in many other areas, which have all contributed to ensuring a far better quality of care now than ever before

A pioneering hospital

Although childhood medicine at the hospital has been hugely transformed for the better during its history, there is a sense in which much of its initial philosophy has remained the same. The central aims of the institution have certainly not changed since they were originally outlined: the treatment of children, the advancement of childhood medicine, and the education of doctors, nurses and the wider community about child health.

The founder of Great Ormond Street Hospital, Dr Charles West, began his work on the advancement of childhood medicine before the hospital was opened, with his published work on childhood diseases. His *Lectures on the Diseases of Infancy and Childhood*, published in 1848, was at the time the most authoritative study of childhood disease in the English language, and it set the scene for future achievement at the hospital. Almost a century later, in 1946, the foundation of the Institute of Child Health (now part of University College London) significantly modernised Great Ormond Street Hospital's approach to research. And in the 21st century, as the only biomedical research centre for childhood medicine in the UK, Great Ormond Street Hospital and the UCL Institute of Child Health together are uniquely placed to provide a world-class environment for research that will no doubt continue to deliver groundbreaking developments.

Childhood specialisation

Arguably the most significant first step that paved the way for all others in childhood medicine in Britain was the beginning of specialisation. Great Ormond Street Hospital made an important contribution to this development. After it opened its doors in 1852, many other children's hospitals were soon founded and the treatment of children in dedicated hospitals started to become widespread across the country. The middle of the 19th century had witnessed a major change in the way that childhood and children were perceived in society, and they now began to be better valued than had previously been the case. This found expression in a succession of new labour and education laws passed in Parliament, designed to protect children from primitive exploitation and to ensure they had opportunities

for learning. But there was still much opposition to the foundation of a children's hospital in London.

With children now regarded as being in a separate category from adults, both in society in general and in medicine in particular, there was more opportunity to concentrate on the diseases specific to childhood. But so limited was the knowledge of childhood medicine in 1852 that in many cases it was not understood what these childhood diseases were. Hence one of the major aims of Great Ormond Street Hospital was to give doctors the opportunity to observe the progress of these conditions in children in hospital, so they could be accurately described and defined. This would open the way to developing more specific and more successful treatments. If a patient died, a post mortem was conducted at the hospital so that medical staff could ascertain whether their diagnosis had been correct, and examine the effects of the disease on the body of the child. This was extremely valuable in understanding the condition that had caused the patient's death. As Dr Andrea Tanner, historian and assistant archivist at Great Ormond Street Hospital, has written, this would allow medical staff 'to build up a picture of the progress of fatal conditions that had hitherto been invisible to the doctors'.

Naming diseases

Charles West used this information in his continued study of childhood diseases, and new members of the medical staff at Great Ormond Street Hospital also began to contribute to groundbreaking research. The first of these were WH Dickinson, who wrote extensively on childhood kidney conditions, and Walter Cheadle, who published articles in the medical press in a number of fields, including childhood rheumatic disease and infantile scurvy. His work on scurvy was continued by his one-time junior, Thomas Barlow. In 1894, the disease was named after Barlow. He had shown that childhood scurvy was no different from adult scurvy, and that rickets was not an essential part of the disease. This era of medicine was characterised by conditions being named after the physician who first managed to isolate and describe their symptoms.

Gee's disease was described in 1888 by one of Barlow's near contemporaries at Great Ormond Street Hospital, Samuel Gee. This was the first recorded account of what is now known as coeliac disease. This is a chronic condition that is characterised by the inability of the digestive tract to process gluten. Unlike many other conditions, such as scurvy and diphtheria, which were common in the 19th century but have very low incidence today, coeliac disease remains a fairly common diagnosis in the 21st century. Gee was ahead of his time in realising that the only way in which coeliac disease was likely to be managed was through diet, though significant steps towards describing the correct diet for coeliacs have only been made in the last fifty years; one of Gee's main dietary recommendations was to eat mussels!

Frederic Still was the third of four Great Ormond Street Hospital physicians who have had conditions named after them (the fourth being Frederick Batten), when in 1896 he described a particular form of juvenile rheumatoid arthritis which has been known ever since as Still's disease. His paper was published in 1896, and was seen as a classic of its kind. In it he described twenty-two patients, all of whom had been seen at Great Ormond Street Hospital. He differentiated in clinical and pathological detail the condition he had observed in the children, as opposed to the broadly similar disease found in adults. Still, who is often called 'the father of British paediatrics', also wrote extensively on a number of other childhood conditions in publications that included his book *Common Disorders and Diseases of Childhood*. As the first full-time paediatrician he could be said to stand shoulder to shoulder with the founder of the first children's hospital, Charles West, and the first

Lister's carbolic spray and antiseptic techniques had a significant impact in reducing post-surgical infection

full-time paediatric surgeon, Denis Browne. All three men had an enormous impact on childhood medicine, not just in Britain but the world over.

Advances in nursing

But the work of these 'big names' of medicine forms only part of the story of the innovation that has taken place, as Great Ormond Street Hospital has also been at the forefront of developments in nursing since the 1850s. Charles West's book on nursing preceded the recommendations of Florence Nightingale, and was explicit in its message that nursing must be modernised in order to serve fully the best interests of patients. When in 1878 the Charles West School of Nursing was founded, Great Ormond Street Hospital established itself as a major centre of childhood nurse training. This role has continued to the present day, and is now fulfilled in association with South Bank University. The highly specialised nursing at the hospital today makes Great Ormond Street Hospital a centre of excellence in many fields, and often an extremely innovative one, too. One

example was the application in 2006 for a patent for a specialised nursing tool developed at the hospital, called GOSHman PANDA, designed to gauge the level of nursing care a child will need.

The medical school

The opening of the Great Ormond Street Hospital medical school in 1888 formalised the nature of the training offered at the hospital. With many eminent names in medicine and surgery working at the school, it became widely known as an international centre of excellence in research and teaching. More general advances in medicine at this time were revolutionising both diagnosis and treatment in hospitals, and ushering in a new generation of doctors who were moving on from the idea that doctors were 'gentlemen first and scientists second'. The advent of the X-ray and the newly founded laboratory both brought great new potential for the medical staff. In his memoirs Dr Poynton records one particular member of staff who was often 'lost in an abstruse problem in a test tube'. His name was Archibald Garrod.

The artificial respirator, or 'iron lung', was one of the many major technological innovations in medicine in the early 20th century

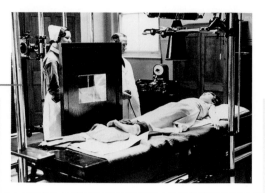

A patient has an X-ray taken at the hospital in the 1930s

From the perspective of the present, it seems that of all the advances made in childhood medicine at Great Ormond Street Hospital before the Second World War it is probably Garrod's that stands out as the most important. This is because not only was he so far ahead of his time, but also his outlook has formed the basis of many exciting areas at the forefront of medical research today. The book of his lectures on the *Inborn Errors of Metabolism* has the same concern with discovering the biochemical and genetic causes of congenital (inherited) abnormalities as modern research in genetics, and is relevant to many different specialisms dealing with inherited disease, from immunology to metabolic medicine. The 'inborn errors of metabolism', a phrase which Garrod had coined,

became a commonplace idiom in the medical world; there was even a Society for the Study of Inborn Errors of Metabolism founded in 1963.

Surgery

By the early years of the 20th century, surgery had benefited from the rapid pace of progress since the 1850s, both at Great Ormond Street Hospital and in the wider world of surgery. Lister's antiseptic technique was one important development, but it was the aseptic technique that gained widespread approval and which has survived today as the safest form of surgical protocol. At Great Ormond Street Hospital and at Guy's Hospital, William Arbuthnot Lane was a pioneering practitioner of the aseptic 'no-touch technique', or Lane technique, that was a rigorous process of the internal fixation of a splint to a broken limb to achieve the best possible alignment. He was also a leading surgeon in cleft-palate and ear, nose and

INBORN ERRORS OF
METABOLISM

The Croonian Lectures delivered before
the Royal College of Physicians
of London, in June, 1908

By
ARCHIBALD E. GARROD
D.M., M.A. OXON.

*Fellow of the Royal College of Physicians,
Assistant Physician to, and Lecturer on Chemical Pathology
at St. Bartholomew's Hospital.
Physician to the Hospital for Sick Children,
Great Ormond Street*

" ἐν πᾶσι τοῖς φυσικοῖς ἔνεστί τι θαυμαστόν."
Aristotle, Περὶ ζῴων μορίων, I. 5.

LONDON
HENRY FROWDE   HODDER & STOUGHTON
OXFORD UNIVERSITY PRESS   20, WARWICK SQUARE, E.C.
1909

Garrod's lectures were ahead of their time; indeed, most of his contemporaries did not realise the significance of his findings

Throat surgery shortly before the outbreak of the First World War

throat procedures, which remain a key feature at the hospital today.

Denis Browne was pre-eminent among the next generation of surgeons, and was globally recognised as a pioneer in a number of fields of paediatric surgery. During his working life the sophistication of anaesthetics improved greatly, allowing more complicated procedures to be carried out. Browne's was an individual brilliance that achieved many astounding results, but it was perhaps the multi-disciplinary team approach of cardiac surgeon David Waterson and cardiologist Richard Bonham-Carter in the 1950s and 1960s, that was even more influential in providing a blueprint for the future.

Team work

The team method of working expanded the model of care for each patient beyond an individual consultant or surgeon to a more general management regime, that often involved other disciplines, such as psychological medicine. This in turn derived from a more holistic appreciation of the patient's needs. Team working extended not only to patient care but to research as well. Modern research teams, augmented at the hospital from 1946 by the UCL Institute of Child Health, have in the main superseded the brilliant individual doctors of the past, such as Still, Barlow and Gee. This is not to suggest that there is no place for individual excellence any more – clearly there is – but the vast resources and skills required for pioneering research are generally better provided by teams (often consisting of laboratory scientists, nurses, pharmacists, psychologists, doctors and others) than by individuals. The team approach

The 'electrical department' in 1905

to both treatment and research, allied to improvements in technology and drugs, has brought great leaps forward in all disciplines of medicine since the Second World War.

For example, under the stewardship of Waterson and Bonham-Carter, the fatality rate for infants with acute heart disease was reduced from 75 per cent in 1955 to 35 per cent in 1973 (the figure now is one to three per cent, depending on the condition). The key technological development that made this remarkable statistic possible was the invention of the heart and lung machine, that allowed the heart to be stopped while surgery took place; major advances in drugs led to more sophisticated anaesthetics for cardiac patients; while team working was a particularly vital factor in cardiac intensive care. The human factors of care were a key concern of Professor Marc de Leval, cardiac surgeon at Great Ormond Street Hospital between 1974 and 2006, who did pioneering work on the impact of human error on cardiac patients. This work led to a collaboration between the cardiac team at Great Ormond Street Hospital and both the McClaren and the Ferrari Formula 1 racing teams. The success of Formula 1 racing is all about crucial attention to detail, and the hospital team was able to learn a great deal from the well-rehearsed procedures and communication techniques applied at crucial pit-stops during a race. They applied these lessons learnt to their 'handovers' where the patient is transferred from one team to another, such as the handover between the surgical team and the intensive care team.

Congenital disease

Paediatric cardiology is just one of many of the 'sub-specialities' that have developed in the modern era of medicine, as childhood medicine, itself so radical a specialism in 1852, has been subdivided into ever more specialised fields. Almost all these different fields, however, have shared to a greater or lesser extent an interest in congenital, or inherited, conditions. Although many of the congenital diseases that are treated at Great Ormond Street Hospital are extremely rare, together they are the single largest killer of children in Britain (traffic accidents are second). So research into understanding and treating these conditions has been an important part of the work of most specialities at the hospital for a number of years.

Andrew Williams (left) and Joshua Perry-Pope (right), respectively the first and 1,000th successful bone marrow transplant patients at Great Ormond Street Hospital

One of the most important recent areas of research has been in trying to isolate and understand the function of the genes responsible for different types of inherited illness and malformation.

Modern genetics has improved medical understanding of congenital conditions and, in some cases, has led to the development of remarkable new treatments. One such pioneering treatment at Great Ormond Street Hospital was gene therapy. This treatment, which attracted global attention, was first used in 2001 on Rhys Evans, a boy who was born with severe combined immunological deficiency (SCID) that left his body unable to withstand attack from viruses and bacteria. In 2005 the Wolfson Centre for Gene Therapy of Childhood Disease was opened, to enable further progress with this exciting area of work. The conventional treatment for this type of condition is a bone marrow transplant, though there is not – as in Rhys's case – always a suitable donor available. This is also used to treat a variety of other, non-congenital conditions including leukaemia and solid tumour cancers. The first successful bone marrow transplant, or BMT, at Great Ormond Street Hospital and in the UK, was performed in 1979 by Professor Roland Levinsky, and in 2007 the thousandth transplant was successfully carried out. Approximately seventy patients a year continue to receive this potentially lifesaving treatment. Two beneficiaries of BMT were Oscar and Alexander Chan, twins who suffered from a rare immunological condition. The BMT centre at Great Ormond Street Hospital is the largest centre of its kind in the UK, and has been at the forefront of innovation in this field since 1979. In 1998 Great Ormond Street Hospital became one of the first hospitals in the world to carry out 'mini BMTs' for children too ill to have a conventional transplant.

Rhys Evans – life outside the bubble

Rhys Evans made international headlines in 2001 when, aged eighteen months, he became one of the first people in the world to be treated with gene therapy. His treatment was described at the time by his mother, Marie, as 'nothing short of a miracle'. And as this book goes to press some six years after his treatment, Rhys remains a healthy boy, able to go to school and play with his friends. That might not sound like much, but it is actually an extraordinary feat for someone with Rhys's condition who has undergone such a pioneering treatment.

As a baby Rhys was diagnosed with rare X-linked severe combined immune deficiency (X-SCID). A defect on the gamma c gene on the X chromosome leaves sufferers unable to produce lymphocytes, the white blood cells that are essential for fighting infections. The disease could not be treated at all until bone marrow transplant, or BMT, became an accepted form of treatment in the late 1970s. Before that time, some patients were kept permanently in a sterile environment, to protect them from infections that their genetically weakened immune systems would not be able to fight. Cases such as that of David Vetter in the USA were high profile, and children with the condition were labelled 'bubble boys'. Inevitably, being kept apart from direct human contact was psychologically damaging for these patients.

BMT was a major step forward, but the technique requires a donor and it is not always possible to find a correct match. Without a transplant, however, children with SCID rarely survive beyond two years old. Rhys had no siblings, so finding a closely matched donor was unlikely. A team decision was made to attempt gene therapy.

The gene therapy treatment was supervised by Professor Adrian Thrasher. A sample of Rhys's bone marrow was

A pioneer in medicine, Rhys was never expected to survive beyond two years old

removed and from it was extracted the stem cells from which the immune system is generated. The cells were then mixed with a retrovirus that 'infected' the cells with a good copy of the gamma c gene that was faulty in Rhys. The final step was to reintroduce the modified cells into Rhys's blood. Within just a fortnight Rhys's immune system was beginning to respond.

Professor Thrasher and his team are the first to admit that as a new form of treatment this cannot yet be called a cure. Rhys will require follow-up for the rest of his life, to check on his progress. Nonetheless, the signs to date have been highly encouraging. 'We were ecstatic about his progress,' said Professor Thrasher. 'We'd been working on the technique for years in the lab, and it was great to take that work into the clinic and see therapeutic success.'

The implications of the long-term success of gene therapy are enormous. Faulty genes underlie many types of conditions, and there is hope that gene therapy could be used in the treatment of numerous congenital (inherited) diseases.

Since Rhys was treated, gene therapy has been used for fourteen further patients at Great Ormond Street Hospital with three different forms of SCID, and the results have been extremely promising. The hospital is currently one of only four centres in the world capable of offering gene therapy to children suffering from life-threatening immune system diseases. Further research has begun to explore gene therapy for inherited blindness in children and for progressive age-related blindness in adults.

The treatment has certainly had a profound impact on Rhys and his family. His father says that Rhys 'lives a pretty normal life; he's a regular kid,' while his mother has no doubt that gene therapy has transformed all their lives for the better. 'We do all the things that other families do – go on holiday, play in the park. Things that would have been impossible without the miracle work of Great Ormond Street Hospital.'

Professor Adrian Thrasher broke new ground with gene therapy treatments

Professor Philipp Bonhoeffer has revolutionised cardiology with techniques that require little intervention

Many breakthroughs

Great Ormond Street Hospital has become a centre of excellence in many other forms of treatment, including craniofacial and neurosurgery, epilepsy, cleft lip and palate, bladder reconstruction and kidney failure. It is clear that there is no sense of complacency anywhere in Great Ormond Street Hospital; there is instead a passionate commitment across all the specialisms to developing and delivering improvements in understanding and treatments.

The amount of groundbreaking work being done today at Great Ormond Street Hospital and the UCL Institute of Child Health is far too great to detail in this book, beyond a very few examples. In 2006, Evelyn Huddy benefited from a pioneering form of keyhole surgery at Great Ormond Street Hospital after she had been

diagnosed with a rare condition called hyperinsulinism. Professor Philipp Bonhoeffer has revolutionised both childhood and adult cardiology through the invention of a non-invasive way of replacing a heart valve without the need for major surgery.

Great Ormond Street Hospital is one of only two centres in the UK to provide surgery for children born with bladder exstrophy. Kirsteen Lupton was one of the patients who benefited from this treatment, and she has since gone on to raise an enormous amount of money for the hospital.

The UCL Institute of Child Health has many researchers working on areas ranging from the use of stem cells to regenerate cells damaged by disease, to large-scale studies of infant mortality and public health measures in both Britain and the developing world. The population health sciences department, that is responsible for these studies, was the first such department in Britain, established in 1986. It is unique among childhood population health departments in having been awarded prestigious Medical Research Council Centre status in 2005. The neural development unit at the Institute has done significant work on the

Alex and Oscar Chan

'I'm just so relieved to see that Oscar and Alex are cured,' said Dr Alan Chan, who is not only the father of his twin boys but their bone marrow donor as well and, by remarkable coincidence, a scientist with a special interest in immunology. Alex and Oscar were diagnosed with an extremely rare inherited condition called Wiskott-Aldrich Syndrome (WAS), after they developed eczema and repeated nose bleeds soon after their birth in 1998. The condition, which affects just four children in a million, is a primary immune deficiency syndrome which occurs only in boys. It is life threatening because the body cannot fight infection, the consequence of low white blood cell (lymphocyte) counts that result from a faulty gene. Sufferers have a particular susceptibility

to problems such as ear infections and pneumonia, which can prove fatal.

The only known cure for WAS is a successful bone marrow transplant, or BMT, that enables the patient's immune system to fully recover by producing its own lymphocytes. The Chan twins have parents from Chinese and Slovenian backgrounds, and this meant that the required donor was always going to be hard to find. Intensive efforts to find a donor through the Internet

and the media ultimately failed, so the team at Great Ormond Street Hospital, led by Graham Davies and Paul Veys, decided to use Alan as a donor for one twin at a time. Alan described the whole experience of the twins' treatment as 'a rollercoaster ride'.

Alex, the more seriously ill of the two boys, was transplanted with marrow from his father in December 1999. The transplant was unsuccessful and had to be repeated a month later, in January 2000. This time the transplant worked, and in June 2001 the BMT team decided to attempt a pioneering 'passage transplant', using Alex as a donor for his twin brother, Oscar. The theory behind this was that the two boys were more similar to each other than their father was to either of them, giving a higher chance of the transplant being accepted by Oscar's body. Once again, however, the first attempt was unsuccessful, and it was only in December 2002 that a successful transplant was made.

After a number of years of treatment, the boys had overcome the odds and survived. Since their transplants they have enjoyed excellent health, and they started school together in 2003. In 2007, aged nine, they were enjoying playing football and had been on their first skiing trip to Europe.

Alex and Oscar are now able to lead active lives after their groundbreaking BMTs

link between maternal nutrition during pregnancy and the health of the child. One study, for example, suggested that an increased intake of folic acid in mothers before conception and during early pregnancy enormously reduces the risk of the unborn child developing conditions such as spina bifida. A study by Dr Atul Singhal and Professor Alan Lucas from the nutrition department established, in an article published in the *Lancet*, that breast-fed infants have a lower risk of coronary heart disease in adult life than bottle-fed babies. There are innumerable examples of important research that have been undertaken and that in many cases will lead to major benefits for child health and the treatment of serious childhood illness.

A global effort

The UCL Institute of Child Health and Great Ormond Street Hospital enjoy a symbiotic relationship. The patients at the hospital benefit from the high level of research expertise at the Institute, which gives them access to the most up-to-date forms of treatment, and the Institute's research work is informed by data from the patients. Many of the researchers are practitioners as well, and the Institute and Great Ormond Street Hospital have together been able to attract many of the most eminent people in the world in their fields. They come because of the excellent track record in high-quality research work and because of the relatively large number of patients with unusual conditions. Having the very best people from many different countries encourages global collaboration to achieve the highest-quality research outcomes. The work in London would often not be possible without a multi-centre effort with other researchers, hospitals and universities from around Britain and the world.

Professor Elliot (right) and Rageh Omar (left)

Dr Bobby Gaspar is working closely with colleague Professor Adrian Thrasher on gene therapy treatments

New challenges

The 21st century has already delivered much innovation at Great Ormond Street Hospital. Treatments such as the gene therapy given to Rhys Evans have captured the public imagination, offering a combination of exciting developments in science and the dramatic impact those developments can have on a child's life. This recent work forms part of the long story of groundbreaking research conducted at the hospital since its beginnings in the middle of the 19th century. Perhaps surprisingly, though, success can bring its own challenges. With a massive increase in the survival rates for major surgery, for example, the expectation of what can be achieved also increases. What was groundbreaking twenty years ago is now regarded as a standard service with a minimal failure rate, so new ways have to be found to improve the service being offered – such as further work on the long-term quality of life of the patient. This is how treatments evolve, and the staff at Great Ormond Street Hospital are eager for success so they can find solutions to new challenges. In the final chapter, this book will look more closely at some of the medical challenges and exciting opportunities facing Great Ormond Street Hospital in the future. But it seems certain that, as long as there is sufficient funding, many more medical breakthroughs will be made at the hospital that will ultimately benefit thousands more sick children.

Leanne Pannell

Leanne Pannell was an extremely fit and active child, and a keen gymnast, before she developed a rare and life-threatening condition when she was thirteen years old. The condition, called idiopathic or primary pulmonary hypertension, narrows the blood vessels in the lungs and puts pressure on the heart. Pulmonary hypertension is extremely rare and difficult to diagnose. For Leanne it took a year of tests until a diagnosis was confirmed at Great Ormond Street Hospital. The condition affects only two people in a million, but can strike at any time, without warning.

Leanne's treatment as an outpatient until she was aged eighteen was supervised by Great Ormond Street Hospital's Professor Sheila Haworth. She was able to prescribe Leanne with a combination of drugs which Leanne could administer herself. The drugs were able to contain the disease, but without any cure for the condition ultimately Leanne may need a lung transplant. This is a high-risk procedure that usually carries with it a limited life expectancy. Leanne has always been aware of these facts, and knows that her long-term prognosis is not good, but she says that she has 'always had such a positive outlook. Without it I would not have been able to lead any kind of life with this condition.'

To date, the innovative combination of four drugs has successfully contained the disease. Leanne has to take tablets every day, but she also has to have a drug pumped into her system continuously, delivered through a needle inserted under the skin on her stomach. The needle has to be moved slightly every few days to keep the drug infusing efficiently. This is extremely painful, because in addition to the discomfort of inserting a needle the drug stimulates pain-detecting nerves in the skin. The alternative is a Hickman line, a semi-permanent catheter which goes through the chest wall to the heart. This is pain free but more conspicuous, and Leanne has wanted to try to lead as normal a life as possible, despite the restrictions that inevitably accompany her disease. In many ways she has been extremely successful in achieving this, for example she passed twelve GCSEs all with A and B grades and progressed to A levels in psychology and sociology. Outdoor activities rate highly with her, too: 'I love to be driving in my car with girlfriends when it's lush and hot, with the windows down and the system up.'

'I have to treat every day like it's my last,' says Leanne. 'Some days I wake up and feel great and full of energy, while some days I can't even get out of bed. Everyday things like walking up the stairs can be extremely hard.'

When Leanne's health declined in 2006, Professor Haworth decided to give her a nebuliser in addition to the skin infusion, so that she could breathe the drug into her lungs in a fine mist. Leanne has been very pleased with the result of this, which has given her more energy: 'I'm the best I've ever been,' she said in 2007. It is hoped that the

combination of medicines will continue to help Leanne lead as full a life as possible and delay the need for a transplant.

'I love to be driving in my car with girlfriends when it's lush and hot.' Treatment has changed Leanne's life, enabling her to do things that would have been otherwise impossible

Amanda says that her time as an inpatient at Great Ormond Street Hospital gave her the energy and determination to become a successful actress

Actress Amanda Redman came to the hospital as a young child suffering from burns.

In the early 1960s, at the age of three, I pulled a pot of boiling soup over myself and received severe burns over my whole body. I was taken to the best children's hospital in the world, both then and now — Great Ormond Street Hospital. More than thirty-five years later, my own daughter, Emily, was a patient at the hospital and also received excellent care.

The severity of the burns I received meant that I required skin grafts. I was treated as an inpatient for a couple of months, and then followed up as an outpatient. As a very young child I do not remember much about my time at the hospital, but I do have very clear memories of looking out from my cot and of the kind nurses who worked on the ward. There is one young nurse I particularly remember, who would come and sing songs to all the patients.

I received the best possible treatment available at the time, though I gather that the progress of medicine has made today's techniques far superior to what I had done, more than forty years ago.

My injuries helped to motivate me to become an actress. I think that being an inpatient for a long period of time gave me a lot of energy and determination to be able to do this. I achieved my ambition, despite the scar on my left arm that some people might have seen as an obstacle to being a successful actress.

Great Ormond Street Hospital helped me with that process, and I am extremely grateful to them for the care that was given to both myself and to Emily.

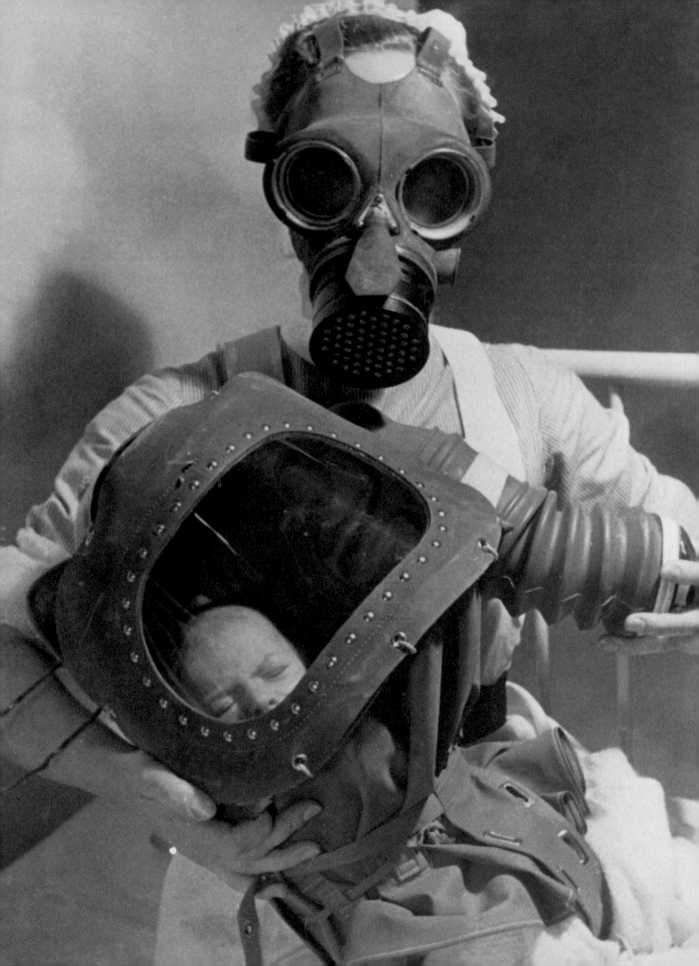

Chapter 5

Wartime

'War is good for babies and other young children.'
Title of a book by Deborah Dwork

Is it possible to be more wrong than to say that 'war is good for babies and other young children'? That surely cannot be true; in fact, in many senses it is demonstrably untrue – children suffer enormously in wartime, not least in major conflicts such as the First World War, because many of their fathers will die. But on a national level, wartime has historically provoked a realisation that investment in the health of children is vital for the health of the country as a whole. This view was recorded in the annual report at Great Ormond Street Hospital in 1915, as the management committee urged that, 'The need for greater effort to counterbalance the drain of war upon the manhood of the nation, by saving infant life for the future welfare of the British Empire, compels the committee to plead most earnestly for the national work this hospital is performing in the preservation of child life. The children of the nation can truthfully be said to be the greatest asset the Kingdom possesses.'

The impact of war on children's lives in Britain has been enormous, but in many ways war has exerted a beneficial impact in the long term development of services for children

The need for healthy children

In the vast human tragedy that was the First World War, there was a constant need for more young men to be sent to the front lines, and in the harsh final analysis healthy children were needed to provide that replenishment. Indeed, in 1916 the hospital's annual report stated, 'It is now universally recognised that there is no ultimate need of the State greater, more imperative or more urgent, than that of securing the health and physical efficiency of the coming generation.' During the Second World War, meanwhile, the decision was made for institutes of child health to be founded. This led directly to the establishment of the Institute of Child Health at Great Ormond Street Hospital in 1946. War may be bad for children, but it invariably seems to encourage initiatives designed to improve their welfare.

The subject of this chapter is the hospital during war and other crises such as terrorism (the bomb attacks on London of 7 July 2005), natural disaster (providing expertise and resources) and disease across the world (engaging in research and preventative action).

The First World War

The First World War brought many challenges for Great Ormond Street Hospital. In 1914 the hospital was used for treating the children of French and Belgian refugees. With the increasing prioritisation of health services for children during the course of the war, the hospital found there was more competition, particularly for the recruitment of staff. This was already a considerable difficulty, as ten of the medical staff had been called up for military service in 1914. Throughout the war nurses were in demand on the western front. The hospital developed two new strategies to deal with the shortfall in medical staff, as recorded in the annual report of 1915:

'The question of filling the vacancies on the Resident Staff for the past year has been an anxious one. For the first time since the foundation of the hospital in 1852, Medical Women have been elected to resident medical and surgical appointments, and the committee note with pleasure the satisfactory manner in which these women have carried out their duties.

The hospital relied heavily on what the committee of management called 'colonial medical men' during the First World War. This picture from 1919 includes Canadians Norman Bethune (back row, second from right) and founder of the British Paediatric Association, Donald Paterson (back row, far left)

Female doctors were absolutely essential for the hospital to continue to run smoothly during the First World War. This picture of the medical staff is from 1917 and includes female doctor Miss Marjory Blandy (front right)

The committee also report their deep sense of obligation to the several Colonial Medical Men who have held and are holding responsible resident appointments in the Hospital since the outbreak of the War.'

Women remained on the medical staff at the hospital until 1919, when they were banished again until the late 1930s. Only then were women allowed to be doctors and surgeons at Great Ormond Street Hospital. In 1916, Miss Naomi Tribe, Miss CR Paterson, Miss HR Lowenfield and Miss Marjory Bland were among those on the resident staff. The 'Colonial Medical Men' that the annual report refers to were principally Canadians, many of whom stayed at the hospital into the 1920s and 1930s. They included Donald Paterson, founder of the British Paediatric Association, who first worked at the

hospital in 1919. Norman Bethune was another Canadian who served at the hospital. He died in China in 1939, and Mao Tse-Tung penned a famous tribute to him in which he wrote that, 'We must all learn the spirit of absolute selflessness from him.'

The line of fire

The hospital was not under the same level of threat in the First World War as it would be in the Blitz twenty-five years later, although bombing raids by zeppelins caused more than 550 civilian casualties on the British mainland between 1914 and 1918. Bombs were dropped in the hospital garden and in Queen Square, just 100 metres away. The hospital itself, though, avoided a direct hit.

The First World War saw the hospital publicising its work as vital not only for children, but for the wellbeing of the whole of the British Empire

Financial pressures

During the First World War Great Ormond Street Hospital had more prosaic things to worry about, particularly its finances. In 1915 the income of the hospital fell by more than £5,000 compared to 1914. At the same time, prices of many essential provisions, including food, medicines, coal and gas, were rising steeply. This situation worsened through the war years, and was not helped by the increasing competition the hospital faced with new institutions set up to care for children's health. In 1917 the management committee felt the need to issue this reminder of the longstanding importance of the hospital as a provider of treatment for children:

'Various schemes have been publicly announced for the preservation and care of child life, but it seems to be forgotten by some of the advocates of these new enterprises that the Hospital for Sick Children was founded for this very purpose; that it was a pioneer in this important pursuit, and that it has carried on the work uninterruptedly and with ever-increasing efficiency for over sixty-five years.'

Nonetheless in 1920, burdened with £30,000 of debt, the hospital had to concede that 'never, since the hospital was founded, have its managers been confronted by so serious a situation as that with which they are faced today'. The situation led for the first time in the hospital's history to nominal fees being charged for treatment.

The flu pandemic

As if the war itself had not caused enough death and human suffering, the flu pandemic of 1918–19 compounded the misery of the people of Europe, and caused more deaths worldwide than the estimated 19 million people killed during the conflict. Dr Frederick Poynton recalled the events of the pandemic at the hospital:

'I need hardly write that in all my experience I never met anything so disastrous as the great influenza epidemic in 1918. It came after the Armistice, when after four years of war the world had [been] worn out with strain and disaster, and it was world-wide. I had known and myself suffered in the first outbreak of the Influenza in the 1880s.

[...] Many of the patients had a dreadful heliotrope colour from swamping of the lungs by blood-stained exudation, and died within 24 or 48 hours. The sight of sailors and soldiers who had struggled through the war and came back safe dying rapidly of influenza was utterly sombre. I went to private houses to find the patients already dead before I arrived. How I escaped when surrounded by cases on every side, and utterly worn out by the hard work of the war, I cannot imagine. All I knew was that if attacked I could have put up no fight. The disease spread through the hospital, and when three of the Sisters died within a fortnight for the first time I saw our nursing staff on the point of being panic-stricken, but they rallied and stood firm and the wave passed over, leaving us sorrowful and short-handed.'

The disease was remarkable for particularly affecting young, healthy adults, which meant that the staff at the hospital were more at risk than the children. The records actually reveal that two (rather than the three that Poynton recalls) nurses and four domestic staff died from the flu in 1918–19. The management committee approved payment of the funeral expenses of the six members of staff, at a cost not exceeding £46 and five shillings. Among the student nurses of the time who witnessed these events was Princess Mary, the future Princess Royal, who completed her training as a nurse at Great Ormond Street Hospital between 1918 and 1920. She later became vice-patron then president of the hospital.

Princess Mary, the Princess Royal, trained as a nurse at Great Ormond Street Hospital from 1918 to 1920

German singer and actress Marlene Dietrich paid a visit to Great Ormond Street Hospital in 1936

The Second World War

1936 saw a visit to Great Ormond Street Hospital from the famous German actress and singer, Marlene Dietrich. But tensions between Britain and Germany were already running high again, after Germany had reoccupied the Rhineland in March that year.

Princess Tsahai

Later in 1936, Princess Tsahai, daughter of Emperor Haile Selassie of Ethiopia (then called Abyssinia) arrived in London after her country had been invaded by Germany's ally, Italy. She trained and worked as a nurse at Great Ormond Street Hospital from August 1936 until the outbreak of war in September 1939, when she was transferred to Stanmore Hospital on the outskirts of London. Comments made in the nurses' training register note how she 'made a very good, conscientious, reliable nurse – careful in detail – most kind and gentle with the children'. Her supervisor also observed that she 'took her place with colleagues and was popular with them'. She subsequently returned to central London and worked at Guy's Hospital during 1940 and 1941, before she returned home to the newly liberated Abyssinia in June 1941, intending to use the knowledge she had acquired to develop child health services there. Within a year of her return, though, she died of meningitis aged twenty-four. The hospital's annual report of that year recorded the princess's death 'with deep regret'. The report adds that, 'by her untimely death Abyssinia loses a powerful influence in the establishment of a modern and efficient nursing and hospital service. This was a benefit to her country which the princess had very much at heart.' A memorial hospital bearing her name was later established in Addis Ababa, though after the revolution of 1974 it was renamed the Armed Forces General Hospital.

*Princess Tsahai cares for a child
at the hospital in the late 1930s*

*The hospital's nurses formed
a guard of honour for Queen
Elizabeth and King George VI
when they visited in 1938*

A royal visit

Princess Tsahai was almost certainly at the hospital in October 1938 for the visit from the King and Queen, to open what would later become known as the Southwood Building. This new building had wards made up of multiple smaller units, regarded as being both more patient-friendly and vital in combating the risk of cross-infection. It increased the hospital's capacity to 326 beds. The block, which is still in use in 2007, was named the Southwood Building in 1946, in tribute to Lord Southwood of Fernhurst, the hospital's 1939–46 chairman.

*King George VI is greeted by his sister, the Princess Royal, at
the entrance to Great Ormond Street Hospital in October 1938*

*Nurses help to fill sandbags to protect
the hospital from bomb damage*

Staff at the hospital inspect bomb fragments after the direct hits it sustained in September 1940

A casualty clearing station

During 1940, the hospital's remaining patients were evacuated to its convalescent home on the Surrey downs, Tadworth Court, and other temporary accommodation outside London. Great Ormond Street Hospital was to be used as a casualty clearing station for the local adult and child population during the Blitz.

The hospital itself became a victim of the Blitz when the new building (named the Southwood Building after the war) was seriously damaged by bombing on the night of 9 September 1940. Fortunately there were no human casualties. An indication of the extent of the damage caused by the five bombs that dropped in and around the hospital was given by the secretary, Herbert Rutherford, in a report

he wrote soon afterwards. 'Bomb No. 4 dropped in Guildford Street at the extreme end of the Nurses' House extension; hardly a window there remains intact. Two rooms were damaged by fire. The blast here was so powerful [that] pieces of the roadway as large as tea plates were hurled skywards over the Nurses' House, to rest on the roof of the hospital two storeys higher.'

'Nurse on the lookout'. An observation post was erected on the roof of the Southwood Building at Great Ormond Street Hospital

An act of bravery

The hospital may, in fact, have been narrowly saved from complete destruction by the heroic exploits of an elderly stoker, William Pendle. Pendle, who was 67 and a veteran of the First World War, managed to turn off the hospital's flooded and damaged boilers before they exploded. His brave actions were recognised with the award of the George Medal. The London Region Civil Defence Headquarters wrote to Pendle soon after, to inform him of the award:

'We recently drew the attention of the Minister of Health to your gallant conduct on 9 September 1940 when, after a bomb had shattered the furnaces and burst gas and water mains at the Hospital for Sick Children, Great Ormond Street, you proceeded to draw the fires, shut off steam and make all as safe as possible, although waist deep in water before you were able to make your escape.

Mr Malcolm Macdonald felt that your resource and initiative were deserving of high praise and he took steps to bring the matter to the notice of

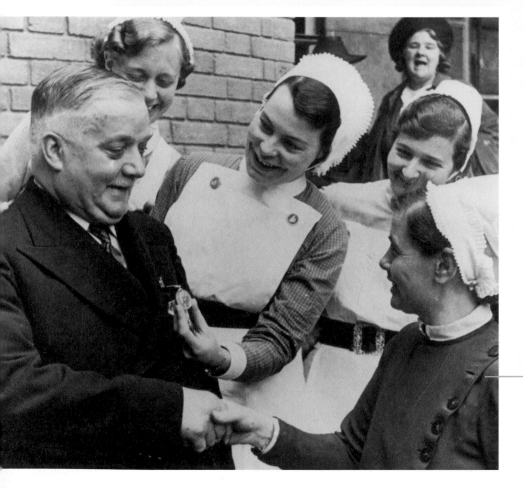

William Pendle shakes hands with the matron, Dorothy Lane, while his medal is admired by other nurses

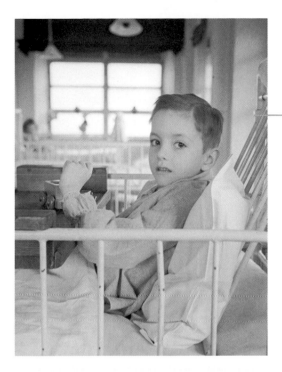

It is likely that Lord Southwood played a leading role in bringing Cecil Beaton into the hospital to take photographs as part of efforts to raise money during the Second World War

a high honour you have won not only for yourself personally but for the Hospital, too, and it will go down in the Hospital's records as a wonderful story of your courage and achievement.'

Lord Southwood

His Majesty the King. We now have the pleasure of informing you, at the request of the Minister, that his Majesty has been graciously pleased to award you the George Medal in recognition of the courage which you displayed.'

Pendle was awarded the honour by the King on 27 May 1941, at a ceremony in Buckingham Palace. Lord Southwood also sent Pendle a letter of congratulations:

'As chairman of The Hospital for Sick Children, I feel I must write and congratulate you on receiving the award of the George Medal. It is

Lord Southwood himself became regarded by many at the hospital as a hero, and after his death in 1946 recognition was given in the annual report by the Board: 'During the all too few years of his chairmanship,' they commented, 'a crushing adverse balance was converted into a credit balance fully sufficient to relieve us of anxiety over the coming costs of completing the rebuilding.' Lord Southwood's business acumen, along with an untiring work ethic, was legendary in the publishing world of the 1920s and 1930s as he competed, principally with his newspaper the *Daily Herald*, with Lords Beaverbrook and Rothermere for dominance of the newspaper market in Britain. But it had not been an easy or straightforward journey for him. Born Julius Elias in 1873, his father was an unsuccessful shopkeeper who had failed in a number of ventures. Elias's first job

earned him five shillings a week, taking down the shutters and cleaning a cheap jeweller's shop, and he had periods of long unemployment before he found the business where he would remain for the rest of his life.

Southwood arrived at Odhams printing press on his twenty-first birthday and worked without pay for the first few days, running errands, until he was noticed by one of the owners of the business who took him on formally as one of only four members of staff. From such humble beginnings, Elias took Odhams to great things – it became one of the foremost printers and publishers in the country.

One of the most novel and distinctive ideas Southwood adopted for raising money was given to him by Gordon Boggon, who was at that time a member of the board of governors. Boggon hatched his

One of the matchboxes
containing hospital
building rubble caused by
1940 bombing

Look in this box!
It contains a little of the rubble that was once part of The Hospital for Sick Children, Great Ormond Street, before it was bombed. Please, PLEASE help!

Lord Southwood's innovative approach to fundraising included the scheme to send rubble from bomb damage to potential donors, appealing for funds

ingenious plan after the hospital was bombed on 9 September 1940. 'Why not', he said, 'turn the rubble into money? Collect it and broadcast it out with an appeal for funds.' As it was wartime, boxes in which to send out the rubble were hard to come by. Someone suggested using empty matchboxes, so thousands of them were collected, filled with rubble and sent to potential donors across the world. Every matchbox was accompanied by a letter, personally signed by Southwood himself. 'This is a personal appeal,' he is reported as saying, 'and I shan't feel that I'm doing my bit unless I sign every letter with my own pen.'

It is estimated that Southwood raised over £1.5 million for the hospital during his tenure. Very soon after the war, in 1948, the hospital underwent perhaps its most radical transformation of all at the start of a new era in Britain, as it joined the newly created National Health Service.

Terrorism

On 7 July 2005, Great Ormond Street Hospital lost two of its staff in the London bombings, and a further six members of staff were injured.

The hospital also found itself on the front line, treating those who were injured in the two bombs that went off a short distance away, at Tavistock Square and on the Piccadilly Line between Kings Cross and Russell Square stations. It was a day of great tragedy for the hospital, but it was also one when many staff displayed marked courage, compassion, dedication and resourcefulness in extraordinary

On 7 July 2005 two bombs exploded within a few hundred metres of the hospital, including the bus bomb in Tavistock Square. The hospital lost two of its staff in the bombings (photograph: AFP/Getty Images)

The canteen at the hospital was used as a makeshift casualty centre on the day of the 7/7 bombings, admitting 22 patients

cardiac intensive care, saw smoke from the explosion from her office on the eighth floor of the hospital, and noticed scaffolders on a nearby building site racing to the ground. She was not sure what was happening, but she made the decision to go and see if she could help.

As news filtered into the hospital of the events that had unfolded, a decision was made to transform the canteen on the ground floor, eight floors below Angie Scarisbrick's office, into an area for receiving casualties from the explosions. Great Ormond Street Hospital is not what is known as a primary receiving hospital, so it does not have an accident and emergency department, but the realisation that it was the closest medical facility to two of the blasts made it clear to the major incident staff that they had to provide whatever treatment they could. The choice of the canteen was made deliberately, because it was on the north side of the hospital, closest to the blast sites. Mark Goninon recalled that, 'the staff restaurant closely resembled a battlefield

circumstances. One member of staff – Angie Scarisbrick – showed all these qualities to such a degree that she was later awarded an MBE. This was the first time the hospital had treated adult patients since the Second World War.

At 9.20am on 7 July, twenty-four minutes after a bomb exploded on the Underground close to Russell Square station, a call was received at Great Ormond Street Hospital from nearby University College Hospital, advising them that they were activating their major incident plan. The major incident team at Great Ormond Street Hospital, led by Sue Lyons and Mark Goninon, was put on standby. Twenty-seven minutes later a bomb exploded on a bus at Tavistock Square. Angie Scarisbrick, a nurse practice educator in

Angie Scarisbrick

Angie recalls the events of 7 July 2005 as though it were yesterday: a series of sharp snapshots that have not blurred with time. After seeing dazed people emerging from Russell Square station, and then the smoke from the explosion in Tavistock Square, she set off to try to help. Arriving at the police cordon at station, she recalls a policeman saying: 'There's been a bomb. There have been lots of people injured. If you can help that would be great.' She stepped across the cordon and walked into the station.

'The first thing I saw was a man who was completely blackened, and the leg below his left knee was missing,' she remembers. 'There were people lying on the floor; they were too shocked to move. There was only one child there – because the first thing I did was to look for children – and he was about twelve.'

He was uninjured, but shocked. Angie began to check the condition of other people in the station and administer first aid, until she came across a woman whose legs had been terribly damaged in the blast. She was in a bad way. And from then on I was with her. 'She arrested and we had to resuscitate her. There was no one to go to hospital with her. So I got into the back of an ambulance that had come in from outside town and we drove to St Thomas's.' Crossing Westminster Bridge the woman arrested again and Angie had to resuscitate her once more,

before handing her over to the team at St Thomas's.

Angie's determination had saved the woman's life. In recognition of that fact, and the help she gave other people that day, she was awarded an MBE in the 2006 New Year's Honours list.

'I was very pleased and honoured to accept the MBE,' said Angie, though she admits that it has not taken away the terrible memories of a day she says will remain fresh in her mind for a very long time. 'It was a truly dreadful day. I have seen a lot, having worked in a military hospital, but it still shocked me.'

Angie Scarisbrick went to investigate what was happening on 7/7 after seeing commotion and smoke from her eighth-floor office window. She saved one woman's life and was awarded an MBE

hospital, with minor procedures initially being performed on tables until we could get stretchers to the area.' In all, this improvised emergency ward admitted twenty-two adults, two of whom needed to be treated in intensive care, and saw a further eight walking wounded.

'The outstanding memories are of the selfless teamwork that occurred,' said Goninon. 'People responded to requests without complaint and without delay; staff didn't go the extra mile, they went the extra five.'

While the hospital was admitting casualties, other staff in addition to Angie Scarisbrick attended at the scene and had to rush back to the hospital on foot to get supplies for treating the wounded, as communication and transport links were badly affected. They included anaesthetists Mike Sury and Fidelma Flynn, and clinical response nurse Mike Collinson.

'We put up drips, gave people oxygen and comfort,' said Sury. 'Of Great Ormond Street Hospital staff, people got on with things without fuss, and the leaders made the right decisions quickly. I think people should be very proud of themselves, quietly.'

The bomb on the Piccadilly Line that morning claimed the lives of Mala Trivedi, who worked in radiology at Great Ormond Street Hospital, and Nazy Mozakka, who worked in chemical pathology, together with twenty-four more individuals. A roof garden was created on top of the hospital's Octav Botnar Wing in tribute to Mala and Nazy and the other members of staff injured in the bombings.

Global disease

The battle against the suffering that people directly inflict on others has seldom been a part of Great Ormond Street Hospital's work. Instead, the fight against disease and illness of all kinds in children has been, and remains, its more constant preoccupation. The vast majority of this work addresses an enormous variety of conditions seen in British children. Through the UCL Centre for International Health and Development at the Institute of Child Health, though, significant work is also being done in the developing world, particularly on improving people's health, nutrition and development. This has included initiatives on improving infant mortality in Nepal, and HIV prevention and treatment. As a global centre of excellence in one of the richest countries in the world, there is a clear awareness on the part of the hospital and the institute that their expertise can be used effectively in the developing world to improve the health outcomes of children. This has also been helped by the opening of The Harris International Patient Centre at Great Ormond Street Hospital in 2006. The centre treats children with serious and complex conditions from around the world, who do not have access to the care they need in their own country, often paid for by their governments.

Natural disasters

Natural disasters in the developing world, such as the Asian tsunami and the earthquake in Pakistan in 2005, further accentuate the lack of health resources and expertise in those regions. Zahid Mukhtar, a specialist registrar in paediatric surgery at Great Ormond Street Hospital in 2005, flew out to Pakistan to offer his help after a quake measuring 7.6 on the Richter Scale hit a remote and mountainous part of the country in October that year, killing more than 70,000 people. Mukhtar treated the injured brought down from the mountains in a basic field hospital, using the same skills and techniques he used at Great Ormond Street Hospital. 'We were operating in tents set up by the army and local doctors,' he said. 'We were working in medieval conditions. Saving lives was the main priority, organisation was chaotic; we had to treat as many people as possible and make do with very basic surgical facilities.'

Even without war, there is always adversity in places across the world and occasionally, as with the events of 7/7, they can be very close to home indeed.

Zahid Mukhtar, a specialist registrar at Great Ormond Street Hospital, flew to Pakistan to help after the 2005 earthquake there

Winner of the 9–12 patient competition category, Emma Lucas tells her story here.

9–12 winner: Emma Lucas

I was unconscious when the car crash happened but I was told I was put on a bed and transported to Great Ormond Street. I was unconscious for a couple of days after the accident but I had my favourite teddy with me. When I woke up I was very lively and I did lots through the days. I had lots of blood tests but soon I didn't mind having them. I also got christened in hospital. I spent my birthday in hospital. I had a little party and most of the kids on the ward came! I was very lively and I chucked my toys at the nurses and my mum and my dad. Soon I could walk which meant I could go back home!

Great Ormond Street saved my life and I will always remember them for it. Thank you.!

Great ormand Street Saved my life
and i will always remember
them for it ♡

THE END

Thank you!
x

Chapter 6

Writers

'Nowadays I tend more to the idea that we blunder into adulthood, as into a darker, bigger room full of people slightly better able to conceal their failings, inadequacies and fears. With any luck, it is not just me: nobody is really grown up – we are all just children, desperately hoping everyone else will be gulled by our long trousers, eye-makeup or long words.'
Geraldine McCaughrean

Great Ormond Street Hospital's association with major literary figures began with Charles Dickens, within weeks of the hospital's opening, and has continued ever since. It is one of the most fascinating, and perhaps unexpected, features of the hospital's history. But it seems likely that this literary connection is no coincidence. The hospital is in Bloomsbury, after all, a place inseparable from literature. Literary associations might therefore be expected, although actually very few of the Bloomsbury writers had any real connection with Great Ormond Street Hospital. More compelling is the idea that many of the changes in society's attitude towards childhood that paved the way for a children's hospital in the 1850s have also been reflected, even amplified, in literature since that time. It seems that, almost by instinct, the two worlds of storytelling and childhood have collided spectacularly, colourfully and often at the hospital.

*Thanks to his gift of **Peter Pan** in 1929, JM Barrie is perhaps the writer with the most famous link to Great Ormond Street Hospital*

Natural allies

The modern idea of childhood is associated with children's imagination and creativity ('grown-ups', by contrast, are supposed to be responsible and reliable), and the fantasy world that is the natural home of the fiction writer is not dissimilar to the idea of a 'Neverland' which adults consider appealing to children. Children and writers are therefore perhaps natural allies in their attempts to fight off the staidness of adulthood that Peter Pan is so adamantly against – the traps of routine that come with being a grown-up. Writing creates a world of fun and fantasy, and so does the imaginative child. *Peter Pan* is the ultimate expression of this. Is it any wonder, then, that this famous hospital, which provides such exceptional care for children, should have links with so many writers?

A wealth of talent

Charles Dickens and JM Barrie have the most celebrated connections with the hospital, but it is less well known that literary figures including Oscar Wilde, AA Milne, Lewis Carroll,

JB Priestley, Monica Dickens, Margaret Gatty and Robert Bridges also have links. Poets Ted Hughes and Tom Paulin have been involved in fundraising for the hospital. Most recently, Great Ormond Street Hospital commissioned a sequel to *Peter Pan*. *Peter Pan in Scarlet* by Geraldine McCaughrean was published in 2006, to widespread critical acclaim.

Oscar Wilde

Oscar Wilde was a friend and neighbour of Adrian Hope, the secretary of the hospital between 1885 and 1904. Hope secured Wilde as a guest and speaker at the anniversary dinner of February 1888. In his speech, Wilde (who was the 'support act' after the Bishop of Peterborough!) praised the 'spiritual beauty' of the hospital's chapel. He also praised the departing superintendent of the hospital, Miss Wood:

'This hospital has lately lost its superintendent Miss Wood, who presided over the nurses for many years with great success. I have much pleasure this evening in proposing the health of the ladies, and I

Lewis Carroll Memorial

31, PALACE COURT,

May 17th 1898

W.

Dear Mr Hope

I write 2 inform you that the Committee of Lewis Carroll Memorial. having now ceded I invite subscriptions. is in a position to provide the sum of £1000 for the endowment of a Cot in the Hospital (Gt. Ormond St.) in perpetuity

The letter informing the hospital of the decision to fund a cot in the memory of Lewis Carroll

Lewis Carroll

couple it with the name of the new Lady Superintendent, Miss Hicks, to whom I think we all wish every prosperity in the fulfilment of her new duties.'

Wilde is not best known for writing for children, despite being the author of the fairytale *The Happy Prince*, but he is well recognised for his celebrations of youth, particularly in his infamous novel *The Picture of Dorian Gray*. *Dorian Gray*, like *Peter Pan*, suggests the idea of eternal youth, though Dorian himself is certainly not a child. Nonetheless, he is determined never to grow old. Wilde's story emphasises how the image of youth had moved on in the late 19th century, from the high Victorian ideal of childhood embodying a kind of moral purity. Instead, boys in particular began to take on roles as fun-loving hedonists, a new romantic notion of childhood and youth that found clear expression in Peter Pan, who more than anything wants to enjoy himself, regardless of the consequences.

Before the era of Wilde and Barrie, in the late 19th and early 20th centuries, Lewis Carroll had created in 1865 another famous child character, Alice. With her studied good manners and constant willingness to help, Alice is noticeably more the archetypal, well-behaved Victorian child than the somewhat rude and selfish Peter Pan. The original illustrator for *Alice's Adventures in Wonderland*, Sir John Tenniel, was a friend and collaborator of Dickens and cartoonist for *Punch* magazine, which undertook a number of appeals on behalf of the hospital.

Punch magazine raised a large amount of money for the hospital. Its 19th-century cartoonist and illustrator of Alice's Adventures in Wonderland, John Tenniel, was also a supporter of the hospital

THE PALACE THEATRE

SHAFTESBURY AVENUE.

MANAGER

MR CHAS. MORTON

Assistant Manager & Treasurer— Mr. PHILIP YORKE

Programme

OF THE

"PUNCH" MATINÉE

IN AID OF THE

Hospital for Sick Children

(GT. ORMOND STREET.)

THURSDAY, MAY 3rd, 1900.

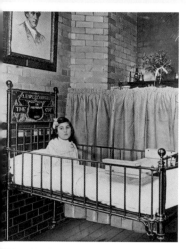

Aunt Judy's Magazine Cot (right) started the trend of sponsoring cots at the hospital; the Lewis Carroll Cot (left) was endowed after the writer's death

Two thousand copies of the first edition of *Alice* were printed, but neither Tenniel nor Carroll were happy with the quality of the printing so they gave many copies away – some to patients at Great Ormond Street Hospital. One thousand pounds of the money raised in Carroll's memory, following his death in 1898, was used to sponsor a cot at the hospital. The tradition of endowing cots had been started in 1868 by another writer, Mrs Margaret Gatty, who was the editor of *Aunt Judy*, a magazine for girls. An appeal to readers of the magazine resulted in the 'Aunt Judy Magazine Cot'.

The Peter Pan League

In 1930, AA Milne and EH Shepard, respectively the writer and illustrator of *Winnie the Pooh*, collaborated to produce a brochure for the Peter Pan League, a club for children that had been

A.A. Milne and E.H. Shepard invited children to join the Peter Pan League to raise money for the hospital

founded to raise money for the hospital. 'Will you join the Peter Pan League and help the Hospital to help other children when they are ill and want comforting?' wrote Milne in the pamphlet. Milne knew Barrie personally and was a member of Barrie's informal, but highly literary, cricket club, the Allahakbarries, who played their final match in 1913 and counted among their number prominent writers such as Arthur Conan Doyle and PG Wodehouse.

The Times

In the early 1930s, author and playwright JB Priestley wrote fundraising articles on behalf of the hospital for *The Times* newspaper, with which the hospital has had many connections. In the 19th century the owner of

THE
PETER PAN LEAGUE

The Hospital for Sick Children
Great Ormond Street, W.C.1

Appeal by A. A. MILNE
Illustrations by E. H. SHEPARD

and included work by a number of writers including a poem called 'The Hospital for Sick Children' by Tom Paulin, about his brother being treated at Great Ormond Street Hospital.

The Times, John Walter, was also chairman of the hospital, and doctors Sir Alan Moncrieff and Dr Jane Collins, who became chief executive of Great Ormond Street Hospital in 2001, have both written extensively for the newspaper. Priestley wrote in a special supplement to raise money for redevelopment in *The Times* in November 1934 that, 'If all is not well for a child, then his enormous reaches of time are a menace... The Hospital for Sick Children exists to protect [children], to conjure back for them those afternoons of sunlight and adventure.'

First and Always

Writing specifically to raise funds for the hospital was an idea emulated in 1988 by poet Ted Hughes, who wrote an introduction for an anthology of poetry called *First and Always*. This was published to contribute to the Wishing Well Appeal,

'It was a startling thing to witness,' wrote Hughes, 'the chain reaction of acts of goodwill which created, in about thirty days, this anthology.'

FIRST AND ALWAYS

Poems for Great Ormond Street Children's Hospital

Compiled and edited by
Lawrence Sail
Introduction by Ted Hughes

Peter Pan in Scarlet

Geraldine McCaughrean's unusual and challenging task of writing the sequel to *Peter Pan*, more than a hundred years after it was first performed as a play in 1904 and almost seventy years after the death of its author in 1937, is described in more detail at the end of this chapter. McCaughrean said of the challenge that, 'I couldn't please everyone, so I think I decided not to try. I settled instead on trying to please Barrie. And myself, of course. Authors are notoriously selfish.' Like Peter himself, perhaps?

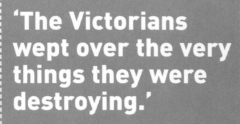

> 'The Victorians wept over the very things they were destroying.'
>
> Peter Ackroyd

Charles Dickens

Charles Dickens is today considered one of the most eminent writers in the English language, but he is also often criticised for being sentimental, indulging in excessive emotion to achieve his artistic aim of affecting his audience. Dickens's writing in support of The Hospital for Sick Children has been described by some as mawkish, and his style often draws attention to the idea that, as Jacqueline Rose wrote in her book *The Case of Peter Pan*, 'Sentimentality about childhood is the other side of guilt.' This is a fascinating but terrible paradox about the Victorian era: while so much was achieved for the welfare of children, poverty, filth and deprivation continued. Children may have been romanticised, but they still endured widespread neglect and abuse, as they still do even today.

Philanthropy

Dickens did not only write about children, however, he was also an active philanthropist with a social conscience. He made a tangible difference to the welfare of children through his support of institutions and through acts of personal charity. The very survival of Great Ormond Street Hospital in its first six years owed much to Dickens, the man whom the *London Journal* described in 1858 as 'from the outset a true and potent friend of the hospital'. His aid was most conspicuous on four occasions: in two articles he published about the hospital in his own magazines in 1852 and 1862, and in two public appearances he made on its behalf in 1858. These appearances raised enormous amounts of money – the equivalent of hundreds of thousands of pounds today – and allowed the hospital to double in size.

A short childhood

Dickens's interest in the fate of children derived partly from the fact that his own childhood was suddenly cut short. His father suffered financial problems, and Dickens was

sent to work on 9 February 1824, just two days after his twelfth birthday, sealing and labelling jars of boot blacking in a rat-infested factory called Warren's, just off the Strand on the River Thames. According to Peter Ackroyd, Dickens's job was 'to cover the pots of paste-blacking: first with a piece of oil paper, and then with a piece of blue paper; to tie them round with a string; and then to clip the paper close and neat all round.'

Soon after he started work at the factory, his father was arrested for debt and Dickens must have felt that his days of happiness had come to an end. But perhaps this sudden ending of his childhood, as Ackroyd suggests, reinforced in his own mind a more romantic notion of the first twelve years of his life. This in turn was one of the factors that made Dickens value childhood so highly for the rest of his life. He used many specific memories from his early years to enliven his fictional work.

Speaking for the hospital

Dickens spoke on behalf of the hospital in 1858, on the anniversary of starting his factory job thirty-four years previously, and he gave what his friend and biographer John Forster

Charles Dickens gave one of his greatest speeches on behalf of the hospital in 1858

described as 'arguably his finest and most powerful address'. The anniversary was unlikely to have been lost on Dickens, who was well known for his keen sense of observation and use of autobiographical detail in his work. Although in his speech he does not refer directly to events from his own childhood, his overwhelming feeling of hopelessness in the factory surely enabled him to convey the image of the pathetic, sick child to his audience. Furthermore, in 1851 Dickens had suffered a personal tragedy – the death of his baby daughter, Dora – that must have reinforced his sense of the vulnerability of children.

The speech was made at the Freemason's Hall on Great Queen Street, Holborn, close to Great Ormond Street. At the time this was the largest non-religious meeting place in the city. Although this was the hospital's first anniversary dinner, it was six years since its opening. The event became an annual event from then on. Many of the guests had supported Great Ormond Street Hospital from the

beginning, such as its president the Earl of Shaftesbury. The 150 male guests sat in the main hall for dinner, while the ladies were restricted to the galleries overlooking the chamber. From here they looked down on the alert and intense figure of Dickens, as he addressed the assembly with his thick, animated voice: 'It is one of my rules in life not to believe a man who may happen to tell me that he feels no interest in children,' he began. In his long and emotional address he went on to describe in detail a sick child whom he came across in Edinburgh, too weak to move and sitting still as though in wonder:

'God knows, I thought, as I stood looking at him, he had his reasons for wondering – reasons for wondering how it could possibly come to be that he lay there, left alone, feeble and full of pain, when he ought to have been bright and brisk as the birds that never got near him – reasons for wondering how he came to be left there, a little decrepit

old man pining to death, quite a thing of course, as if there were no crowds of healthy and happy children playing on the grass under the summer's sun within a stone's throw of him, as if there were no bright, moving sea on the other side of the great hill overhanging the city; as if there were no great clouds rushing over it; as if there was no life, and movement, and vigour anywhere in the world – nothing but stoppage and decay.'

Dickens finished by entreating the guests to contribute generously to the hospital:

'This is the pathetic case which I have to put to you; not only on behalf of the thousands of children who annually die in this great city, but also on behalf of the thousands of children who live half developed, racked with preventable pain, shorn of their natural capacity for health and enjoyment. If these innocent creatures cannot move you for themselves, how can I possibly hope to move you in their name?'

Dickens was, of course, successful in his aim. He moved many of his audience to tears, but they were also moved to contribute generously. The evening raised £2,850, an enormous sum at the time, enough to buy the neighbouring house in Great Ormond Street with more than a thousand pounds to spare.

Dickens had played a significant role at the start of the hospital's history in 1852, when he wrote the article 'Drooping Buds', published in his magazine *Household Words*, which seems likely to have prompted Queen Victoria to become patron of the hospital. In *All the Year Round,* the magazine that replaced *Household Words*, Dickens published in 1862 a further article by Henry Morley that celebrated the tenth anniversary of the hospital and continued its support for an institution still very much in its infancy.

A hero

Dickens's influence on the fortunes of Great Ormond Street Hospital cannot be underestimated. His fame and celebrity in

The articles published in Dickens's Household Words *and* All the Year Round *were seen as such effective pieces in promoting the hospital that they continued to be printed to encourage support*

the English-speaking world was enormous. He was a superstar of his day — greeted by large crowds when he arrived in America, for example — as well as a very well-connected and serious social reformer. He conferred upon Great Ormond Street Hospital not only the immense benefit of his public support, but also a significant amount of money, at a time when it was desperately needed. Criticisms of his sentimentality are valid, but are children not similarly sentimentalised today, albeit not in the same florid Victorian prose? Dickens had the courage and integrity to back up his words with actions, and as a result did an enormous amount to diminish not only the symptoms but also the causes of child suffering in his own lifetime and beyond. He is one of the heroes not only of Great Ormond Street Hospital, but of the welfare of children in general.

JM Barrie and Peter Pan

Great Ormond Street Hospital is famous for two things — making sick children better, and being the second home of Peter Pan, the eternal boy who became a global icon. In 1929, JM Barrie's gift to the hospital of the copyright of

> '**At one time Peter Pan was an invalid in the Hospital for Sick Children in Great Ormond Street, and it was he who put me up to the little thing I did for the hospital.**'
>
> JM Barrie

Peter Pan was a remarkable act of generosity. Peter Pan has become as much a part of the hospital's identity as the very buildings it is housed in. Beyond the fact that the royalties from *Peter Pan* have raised so much money for the hospital, Peter is such an enduring symbol of childhood and an inspiration for sick children that it is hard to think of a more appropriate character to be linked with Great Ormond Street Hospital. So it seems only fitting that this section of the book should look at how the original play came to be written and performed, and the circumstances of Barrie's gift to the hospital.

Barrie and Michael Llewelyn Davies act out a scene from Peter Pan, *with Barrie playing Hook and Michael playing Peter*

It is said of Barrie that he, more than anyone, was the child who would simply not grow up. Characteristically brief remarks in his notebooks from 1878, when he was eighteen, seem to offer evidence of this. 'Greatest horror – dream I am married – wake up shrieking. Grow up and have to give up marbles – awful thought.' Barrie tried his best not to give up the pursuits of childhood; he loved playing games for much of his adult life. In 1890 he founded his own cricket team, the Allahakbarries, which played regularly for the next twenty-three years. He also enjoyed fly-fishing, and devised adventures for children such as playing at pirates in which Barrie was a Captain Hook-like character called Captain Swarthy, 'a dark and sinister figure who displayed despicable cowardice in the face of his young antagonists'.

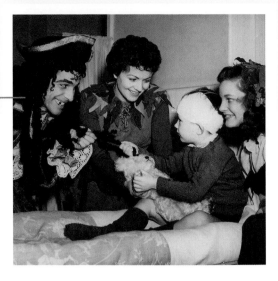

Performances of Peter Pan *were an annual event at the hospital after 1929, and members of the cast would visit the children in costume. Margaret Lockwood (centre) is the actress playing Peter here in the early 1950s*

These games found their way into *Peter Pan*, but other events from Barrie's life also influenced his writing. The death in 1867 of his elder brother, David, in an ice-skating accident, had a major impact on the six-year-old Barrie. His brother would never grow old; at 13 he would remain for ever young. Andrew Birkin, author of *JM Barrie and the Lost Boys* and a friend and benefactor of Great Ormond Street Hospital, wrote that, 'If Margaret Ogilvy [Barrie's mother] drew a measure of comfort from the notion that David, in dying a boy, would remain a boy for ever, Barrie drew inspiration. It would be another thirty-three years before that inspiration emerged in the shape of Peter Pan, but here was the germ, rooted in his mind and soul from the age of six.'

The lost boys

The 'lost boys' of Birkin's book are the real-life inspiration for the lost boys in *Peter Pan* – the Llewelyn Davies children. Barrie had befriended the boys in Kensington Gardens, while walking his enormous St Bernard dog, Porthos (who with his successor, Luath, inspired the character of the dog/nanny Nana, in *Peter Pan*). By strange coincidence, Porthos was named after the St Bernard in George du Maurier's novel *Peter Ibbetson*, and the Llewelyn Davies boys were the grandchildren of

Barrie aged six years old, around the time of his brother's death – 'another boy who wouldn't grow up'

du Maurier. They were George, Jack and Peter, and later Michael and Nico. Barrie ultimately became the guardian of the children after their parents' untimely deaths. He later wrote, in 1928, that *Peter Pan* had been made 'by rubbing the five of you violently together, as savages with two sticks produce a flame.'

The writing of *Peter Pan*

The story and play of *Peter Pan* emerged gradually over a number of years. Peter made his first appearance in *The Little White Bird*, begun by Barrie in 1900 and published in 1902, in a chapter entitled 'Peter Pan in Kensington Gardens'. This told the story of how the baby Peter came to Kensington Gardens and learned to fly from the fairies who lived there. Then, on 23 November 1903, Barrie sat down to write what was to become *Peter Pan*. The working title for the play was *Peter and Wendy*, surprising for at the time there was no such name as Wendy. Barrie did not claim to be the inventor of the name; that distinction belonged to the daughter of his friend WE Henley, Margaret. She called Barrie 'my friendy', but because of her inability to pronounce the letter r it sounded more like 'my wendy'. The name stuck, as did 'Wendy house', which was first used in the play.

By 1 March 1904 Barrie had finished the first draft and was ready to get it produced.

Yo ho heave to A pirating we go

Peter Pan has captured the imagination of many illustrators, and numerous versions of its characters and scenes have been depicted, such as these images by Gwynedd Hudson

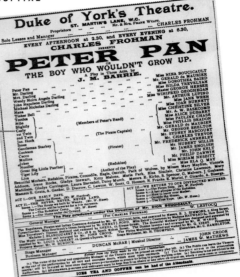

The first production of Peter Pan at the Duke of York's Theatre in London's East End in 1904 was an enormous success

In the absence of his American friend and theatrical producer, Charles Frohman, he first showed the play to veteran London theatre manager, Beerbohm Tree. His reaction was one of astonishment, and he wrote to Frohman in America to warn him. 'Barrie has gone out of his mind,' he wrote, '[he] must be mad.' Birkin's description of the play makes this reaction seem understandable. 'By contemporary standards, *Peter and Wendy* read like a Barnham and Bailey circus extravaganza. Not only did the script require massive sets and a cast of over fifty – to include pirates, redskins, wolves, a lion, a jaguar, a crocodile, an eagle, an ostrich, a dog and a "living" fairy – but at least four of the cast were called upon to fly in highly complex movements.'

When Frohman had returned from New York, in mid-April 1904, Barrie rather nervously took the play to the great Broadway producer, now calling it *The Great White Father*. Frohman was favourably

It is telling that in the story of Frohman's death on the sunken Lusitania *in 1915, he is said to have stood on deck as the ship sunk and asked (in an echo of Peter's bold statement 'to die will be an awfully big adventure'), 'Why fear death? It is the greatest adventure in life'.*

impressed, struck by the play's extraordinary vision, extravagance and adventure. The only thing he did not like was the title, and it was he who suggested it be changed to *Peter Pan*, though Barrie continued making other changes to the play for many years afterwards. Frohman was central to the ultimate success of the play. He gave instructions that no expense should be spared in its production.

On to the stage

The first production of the play was to take place in the Duke of York's theatre and would star, among others, Gerald du Maurier, uncle of the Llewelyn Davies boys, as both Mr Darling and Captain Hook, and an actress, Nina Boucicault, as Peter. At Barrie's behest, preparations for the play were made in the utmost secrecy, even for the cast, none of

whom had complete scripts or knew the full plot.

The curtain rose on the first performance on the evening of 27 December 1904, following rehearsals that had lasted until the early hours of that morning. Frohman waited anxiously in New York to hear news. He was relieved when a cable arrived: 'PETER PAN ALL RIGHT. LOOKS LIKE A BIG SUCCESS.' It was a huge understatement; the audience's reaction was rapturous, and many of the reviews likewise. The review in *The Times* declared that, '*Peter Pan* is from beginning to end a thing of pure delight.' So the phenomenon began. Peter received an even more rousing reception when he first appeared in the United States in 1905, when for example Mark Twain said that, 'The next best play is a long way behind it.'

The gift of *Peter Pan*

It was another twenty-five years before Barrie made his gift of the copyright to Great Ormond Street Hospital. By that time, two of the Llewelyn Davies boys – George and Michael – had already died. It seems this was not a sudden gesture from Barrie, but that he had long thought about how he could help the hospital.

When Barrie first came to London in 1885 he had lived in Bloomsbury, not far from Great Ormond Street. His name appears in the visitor's book in 1901. It seems that he first donated money to the hospital in 1908, possibly because of his connection with the Astor family, who funded a new outpatients building that year. His later bequest to the hospital may also have been partly facilitated by personal connections, as the chairman of the hospital from 1922 to 1927 was Lord Wemyss whose daughter, Cynthia Asquith, was Barrie's secretary and friend. Barrie would

Barrie with Cynthia Asquith, his secretary and friend, whose father Lord Wemyss, had been chairman of Great Ormond Street Hospital

The first performance of Peter Pan *at the hospital in 1929. Barrie watched the performance from the back. He is circled here as the cast perform to the children on Helena ward*

have been well acquainted with the hospital and its work.

The youngest of the Llewelyn Davies boys, Nico, recalled Barrie asking him directly in 1928 if he thought it would be a good idea to give the royalties from *Peter Pan* to Great Ormond Street Hospital. Nico, despite realising that this decision might have an impact on his own personal wealth, agreed that it would be. In February 1929, Barrie was invited to sit on a committee at the hospital. He declined the invitation, in a letter in which he wrote, 'At some future time I might find a way of helping.' Just two months later, in April, the news of Barrie's gift was announced. A number of myths surround the exact circumstances of the events which took place afterwards. One of these says that on the day after the hospital was told of the gift, a lawyer was dispatched to Barrie's house just off the Strand, at 9am, to get the necessary papers signed. After knocking at the door, the lawyer was informed by Barrie's manservant, Harry Brown, that 'Sir James does not rise before eleven'. The lawyer allegedly sat on the doorstep until the hour arrived, when he was finally admitted. Other accounts, however, suggest that Barrie was not even in London at the time.

Supporting the hospital

What Barrie's gift certainly did was to provide a steady income for Great Ormond Street Hospital and inaugurate Peter as a Very Important Person there. Barrie discreetly attended the first performance of the play in the hospital, in 1929, a tradition that continued for many years. Peter's influence can still be felt in numerous ways at the hospital today, not least because the sequel to his story, commissioned by the hospital, was published in 2006. The amount of money raised for the hospital remains a secret, as requested by Barrie, but although the income has been significant, it alone cannot deliver the full extent of the charitable funds needed by the hospital to remain a world leader in its field. Press reports about the level of income have also, in the main,

07

ST. JAMES'S PALACE,
S.W.1.

April 18th, 1929.

Dear Sir James,

As President of the Great Ormond Street Hospital, I write to thank you most sincerely for having presented to the Hospital all your rights in 'Peter Pan'.

I cannot think of a more appropriate gift to help sick children and, together with all those who have the interests of the Hospital at heart, I am very grateful to you for your happy thought.

Believe me,

Yours very truly,

Edward P.

Sir James Barrie, Bt., O.M.,
   3 Adelphi Terrace,
      W.C.2.

The Prince of Wales wrote to Barrie personally to congratulate him on presenting the hospital with the gift of Peter Pan

been grossly exaggerated. Nonetheless, Barrie's is the greatest gift the hospital has ever received, not only in financial terms but also because Peter is the most vivid reminder of a childhood unconstrained by illness, rules or even adults. That reminder has been, and remains, a very real symbol of hope for the children at the hospital.

Peter Pan in Scarlet

Producing a sequel a hundred years after the original became one of the most iconic stories of its century was always going to be an

The spectacular cover art for Peter Pan in Scarlet, *by David Wyatt*

adventure of a lifetime – and such amazing fun!'

However, even McCaughrean and the hospital could not have anticipated the superb commercial and critical reaction to *Peter Pan in Scarlet* that followed its publication. 'Luckily I did not realise, back then, just how big this book was going to be,' said McCaughrean. 'I did not realise that people all over the world would be buying it.'

A sequel was needed to maintain the funding, as the copyright on *Peter Pan* itself would be coming to an end in 2007. The original copyright had actually expired in 1987, fifty years after Barrie's death, but an unprecedented amendment to the Copyright, Designs and Patents Act 1988, tabled by Lord Callaghan, gives Great Ormond Street Hospital continued right to royalties of the play, books and other adaptations in the UK for as long as the hospital exists.

extraordinary undertaking. For Geraldine McCaughrean, the author chosen to write the story by the special trustees at Great Ormond Street Hospital, it was the beginning of a personal odyssey. 'It is an astonishing, daunting privilege to be let loose in Neverland, armed with nothing but a pen, and knowing I'm walking in Barrie's revered footsteps,' she said. 'But completing this book is going to be the writing

Lord Callaghan's wife, Lady Audrey Callaghan, was the chairman of the hospital (1969–82) and was the key figure in ensuring that this unique amendment was enshrined in law. The debate in the House of Lords that followed the tabling of the amendment was astonishing, particularly for some of the asides that were made, which are unlikely ever to be heard in the chamber again. 'My Lords,' said one peer, 'I must tell my noble friend that one of my greatest friends was Tinker Bell.'

In 1995 new legislation within the European Union standardised the term of copyright to the extent of the author's life plus seventy years, which meant that the copyright for Barrie's works would now expire on 31 December 2007. It was therefore decided by the special trustees at the hospital to hold a competition in 2004, on the centenary of the first performance of *Peter Pan*, for a new work, a novel that would introduce a modern generation of adults and children to the characters and themes of *Peter Pan*, and provide continued funding for the hospital. The competition invited entries from around the world. It was judged by a panel of experts that included David Barrie, JM Barrie's great-great-nephew.

McCaughrean was already the author of 130 books for adults and children. In her entry the judges found something that captured the elusive spirit of the original, in its tone and its appeal to audiences of all ages. However, Geraldine had understood that there were inherent difficulties in writing this sequel. She shared these with the author of this book:

KT: Was starting to write the book a straightforward process?
GM: I faced certain snags, technical and otherwise, in contemplating what I would

Kipper Williams' cartoon in the Sunday Times records the ongoing debate between children and adults

Geraldine McCaughrean at the launch of
Peter Pan in Scarlet *in 2006 with*
JM Barrie's great-great-nephew David Barrie

write. The Darling children and the lost boys came back to London at the end of *Peter Pan and Wendy*. Only Peter stayed in Neverland. So they went on growing up, whereas Peter did not. Barrie pretty much sealed the end of his novel with blanket stitch, glue and a zip. Worse still, the arch villain Hook was last seen disappearing into the gullet of a crocodile, and I don't write ghosts'.

KT: How as an adult do you make your writing appeal to children?

GM: I think it helps that, like Barrie, I feel passionately about the importance of Imagination. Neverland (and I don't just mean the one where Peter Pan lives) is the place you can go when you are unhappy, afraid, worried, or lonely, and know you will feel better about yourself. You can people it with whomever you choose, be brave and clever and marvellous; you can make things turn out as you wish. Actually it is a gift everyone ought to hold on tight to. I hate it when adults talk as if an imagination is something only children need. I still play a lot in my imagination. Maybe that's my 'in' on childhood.

KT: What did you know about Great Ormond

Street Hospital before you started?

GM: I knew of it, and what it did. But ever since the middle of 2006, wherever I go and whomever I meet, there is always some connection with Great Ormond Street Hospital. Someone is an ex-patient of the hospital, the parent of a child who was a patient there, or has, at some stage, worked there. Even overseas, somewhere rural in Canada, I met a boy who had begun his treatment at Great Ormond Street Hospital before his parents emigrated.

It helped also, knowing that this would probably be the single most useful book I would ever write. I cannot help thinking, from time to time, that the work of an author is insignificant in comparison with the work of teachers or doctors or electricians. This time at least, because I was writing it for Great Ormond Street Hospital, it would be of real practical usefulness. For that reason alone, I think JM Barrie would approve.

KT: And how about Peter?

GM: Luckily, I think as one with Barrie on a lot of things. For instance, I find a complex character with a dark side is much more interesting than superhero versus a cartoon villain. I agree that children aren't cherubs so much as anarchists: that [in stories] terrible things ought to befall them as often as possible in the course of their adventures.

Peter Pan in Scarlet was published by Oxford University Press in October 2006. It has to date been printed in thirty-nine editions in thirty-six languages, and is a truly global phenomenon. But it has been not just a commercial success. The critical reception was also overwhelmingly effusive. As Philip Ardagh's review in *The Guardian* said:

'It would be understandable if Great Ormond Street Hospital had gone for glitzy, mass-market appeal. Instead, they have chosen a more sophisticated and subtle approach: a book of timeless charm. This truly commendable decision was probably made easier by the fact that McCaughrean's submission must have blown even its closest rival out of the water. Books such as this are as rare as fairy dust. What McCaughrean has done is nothing short of miraculous. It's enough to make you believe in fairies.'

Tess and Vernon with patients Hannah Stanger-France and Dominic Head

We want to do what we can to keep the 'Great' in Great Ormond Street Hospital. In our role as patrons of the hospital charity we are helping efforts to raise the money needed to maintain Great Ormond Street Hospital as a world leader in children's care. At the moment the money is mainly needed to help rebuild the hospital, so it can provide the best possible facilities and treatments.

Tess Daly and Vernon Kay, successful television presenters, talk about how they became patrons of the Great Ormond Street Hospital Charity.

Tess

I was lucky enough to open The Comfort Zone in the newly built Octav Botnar Wing. It is absolutely wonderful – really light and welcoming – and something like the rest of the hospital hopes to look like after the redevelopment.

We have both visited the hospital a number of times. After the visits I feel some very mixed emotions, including sadness and a real sense of injustice that some children should have to endure so much suffering. But I also come away feeling genuinely inspired both by the children, who never seem to be self-pitying, but are full of determination to get better and have astonishing appetite for life, and by the staff whose commitment and dedication is absolutely amazing.

Vernon

Being a dad has made me very aware of how vulnerable children are, and if something goes wrong it's reassuring to know that in this country we have one of the very best children's hospitals in the world. Obviously, you hope that it won't be your own child who will need the expertise which Great Ormond Street Hospital provides, but it might be. The hospital treats tens of thousands of patients a year with some of the most complicated and serious problems, and more than half of those are from outside London, from all over the country.

The hospital needs more money to carry on improving. We are doing what we can to make sure the charity achieves its ambitious targets for fundraising, so they can deliver the highest quality care in the best possible buildings.

We would also like to implore you to donate whatever you can, so that Great Ormond Street Hospital can not only carry on being 'Great', but become even greater.

£95,000
£90,000
£85,000
£80,000
£75,000
£70,000
£65,000
£60,000
£55,000
£50,000
£45,000
£40,000
£35,000
£30,000
£25,000
£20,000
£15,000
£10,000
£5,000
£0

Chapter 7

Charity

'Of all the leading charitable institutions with which our great metropolis abounds, there is scarcely one of a more interesting character than that in Great Ormond Street, Bloomsbury, which administers to the afflictions of the children of poor parents.'
The *London Journal*, 13 November 1875

Great Ormond Street Hospital's very survival depended on donations from benefactors, subscribers and philanthropists for almost a hundred years before the advent of the NHS in 1948. In these years fundraising was required in order to treat every patient, make every meal and pay every nurse. In the 21st century, by contrast, that basic level of provision is paid for by the state, through the NHS. But in order for Great Ormond Street Hospital to remain a world leader in childhood medicine, developing pioneering treatments and delivering the best possible care and training, charitable fundraising is still required on a massive scale.

Gary Lineker and BBC economics editor Evan Davies at a fundraising event on behalf of Great Ormond Street Hospital in 2006

A continuing necessity

Development and research are two of the main destinations of modern charitable funds. The contemporary approach to raising money at the hospital has been informed by the innovative techniques used in its first century of existence, which included annual fundraising dinners, the sponsorship, or endowment, of individual cots and specific redevelopment appeals. Underpinning all these efforts throughout the hospital's history has been the sick child. When Charles Dickens made his appeal on behalf of Great Ormond Street Hospital at the first annual dinner in 1858, he asked the audience, 'If these innocent creatures cannot move you for themselves, how can I possibly hope to move you in their name?' The plight of sick children does have a massive emotional impact which has moved, and continues to move, many thousands of people to contribute to the hospital. Great Ormond Street Hospital uses that income not only to treat the needs of patients, but also to investigate the causes of disease and to remain at the forefront of efforts to ensure that childhood health remains a priority for successive governments.

Key individuals

Securing enough money to found the hospital at Great Ormond Street was aided by Charles West's foresight in having a number of highly influential supporters from the outset, including the Earl of Shaftesbury, Dickens himself and Dickens's friend, the wealthy philanthropist Angela Burdett-Coutts. The importance of these three in the development of rights for children, and schemes for childhood welfare in general, in the 19th century cannot be underestimated – they were arguably *the* most important figures in bringing about key legislative and cultural changes, and in the actual giving of charity as well. Shaftesbury and Burdett-Coutts were both made life governors of the hospital after they made donations fulfilling the criteria stated in the record of the first public meeting in 1851 that, 'A donation of Thirty Guineas or upwards in one sum, or in several sums contributed within three years, constitutes a Life Governor; and an Annual Subscription of Three Guineas or upwards, an Annual Governor.' With such eminent people seen to be providing support for the hospital, it was clear that many more would follow. This was enhanced further when Queen

Princess Alexandra, the Princess of Wales, receives purses containing donations to pay for the 1893 building at Great Ormond Street

Victoria gave the hospital her public backing and became its patron soon after it opened in 1852.

Subscriptions

Annual subscription was a key form of fundraising. It enabled the hospital administrators to plan ahead, with a dependable source of income. In 1872, annual subscriptions were worth £3,342 to the hospital. In return for their donations, subscribers were entitled to recommend patients who, in theory at least, would have priority over those without a recommendation. In the 1870s this meant, for example, that 'Annual Subscribers of Two Guineas... may recommend One In-patient and Five Out-patients yearly'. The reality, however, was that the doctors increasingly admitted the cases they thought were the most urgent and interesting from a medical point of view; the recommendations of subscribers were often ignored.

In order to encourage subscriptions, visitors were welcomed into the hospital from the beginning. Lady visitors such as Louisa Twining, a philanthropist and friend of Angela Burdett-Coutts, came to view the patients and look over the facilities. They were shown around by the matron, and became a common feature of the hospital even when visiting from parents had been curtailed to just one afternoon a week. Dr Andrea Tanner suggests that visiting was seen by the ladies, at least partly, as an opportunity to teach middle-class values to the working-class children. It is also clear that these visitors had a significant impact on the amount of income received by the hospital. Tanner says that, 'The ladies, in making a visit to the hospital an acceptable part of the metropolitan social round, encouraged others to visit, and greatly increased the subscription list of the hospital.'

Legacies

In 1855 Great Ormond Street Hospital was left money in a will for the first time, when Miss Thompson from Brighton bequeathed £400 to the hospital. The hospital management saw the potential in this for the future, and the annual report of 1856 included an advertisement featuring suggested wording for future bequests. Money raised from legacies has since formed a large part of the income of the hospital, and continues to do so today.

The endowment of cots

In 1868 a cot was sponsored for the first time, through an appeal to the readers of *Aunt Judy's Magazine*, run by Mrs Gatty. The readers raised £1,000, which financed the costs of a bed 'for perpetuity'. It would seem the initiative appealed to the world of publishing as other magazines later also endowed cots, such as The Quiver Cot in 1869,

and The Mr Punch Cot in 1900.

The endowment of cots became increasingly popular, and many individuals and organisations got in on the act. Perhaps the most famous was the Lewis Carroll Cot on Annie Zunz Ward. There were some rather unusual cot names, such as the 'In memory of Algiers Cot' on Louise Ward, endowed with £1,000 in 1878 by legacy of the late Mrs Atkinson Holden. What exactly the 'memory of Algiers' was remains a mystery.

Some cots were also controversial, such as those endowed in the 1920s by notorious arms dealer, Basil Zaharoff. He endowed three cots: the Sir Basil, Helene and Maria del Pilar Cots, the third named after his second wife. Zaharoff was parodied in *The Broken Ear*, a story from Hergé's *Adventures of Tintin* in which he is called Basil Bazarov, works for a company called Korrupt

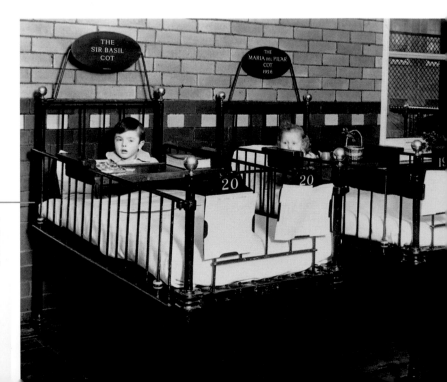

The Sir Basil Cot and Maria del Pilar Cot pictured here were both sponsored by Sir Basil Zaharoff

Arms, and sells weapons to both sides. In the present day such donations would not be possible as the charity has placed strict rules on the type of contributions it is able to receive — weapons manufacturers and tobacco companies are two examples of groups that are not able to contribute to the charity.

The practice of endowing cots ended with the advent of the NHS, but it had in practice already become problematic because the number of endowments had exceeded the total number of beds at the hospital.

Anniversary dinners

Anniversary dinners, which began in 1858 with the memorable speech from Dickens, were also a successful source of fundraising for many years in the 19th century. They often featured notable speakers drawn from the worlds of politics, literature, newspapers and the Church. The occasion became a major annual event in the London social calendar, and remained so until the turn of the 20th century when, according to reports such as those by Dr Poynton, who began working at the hospital in 1900, they lost some of their initial excitement.

'When we read of the Anniversary festivals held to obtain support for Great Ormond Street Hospital, and of Charles Dickens,' wrote Poynton, 'we for a moment seem to drift back to the old Victorian days. I attended one of the last of such dinners, but they were beginning to lose ground.'

Charitable donations

At the beginning of the 20th century, and increasingly after the First World War, the move away from voluntary hospitals supported by charity, towards a state-funded NHS was beginning to acquire momentum. Poynton remarks that 'a good deal was being said about the word "charity", and pressure was showing to declare that our hospitals should not be charitable but national institutions. They should not be used only for the poor, but for all members of the community.' But although since the foundation of the NHS the treatment of patients has been paid for by the government, charitable income has remained vital in order to fund the drive for world-class excellence in every aspect of the work of Great Ormond Street Hospital.

The Royal Family

The royal family has been an important supporter of Great Ormond Street Hospital from its earliest days. Its association with the hospital has taken many different forms, through numerous members of the family. The hospital commemorated its centenary within a week of its present patron, Queen Elizabeth II, celebrating her coronation in February 1952. A hundred years earlier, the Queen's great-great-grandmother, Queen Victoria, became the hospital's first patron soon after it opened and contributed £100 to the new institution. So began a tradition of royal patronage that continued through the reigns of Edward VII, George V and George VI.

Having Queen Victoria's name at the top of the hospital's subscription list provided a great example for other potential subscribers to follow. But as well as providing patronage, Queen Victoria and her family also donated many materially useful things including linen, children's clothes, game meat, vegetables and toys. In 1864, for example, the Queen sent a large gift of toys she had purchased while on a trip to Germany. According to Dr Andrea Tanner, her patronage 'helped to confirm Victoria as the "mother of the people", and Great Ormond Street Hospital as one of her favourite children. This was a very important signal of royal favour, and encouraged the emulation of her gesture among the rest of the hospital's supporters.'

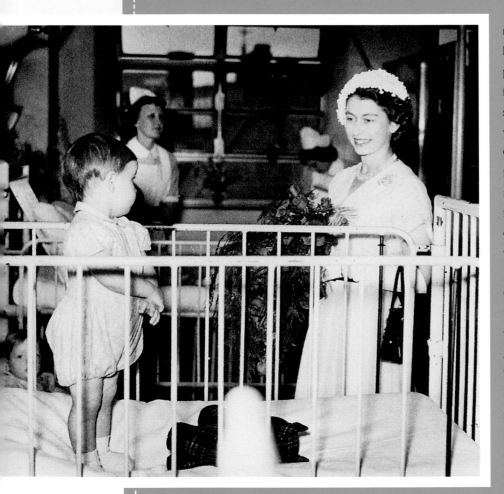

The hospital's patron, Queen Elizabeth II, on her first visit to Great Ormond Street Hospital as Queen in the year of her coronation

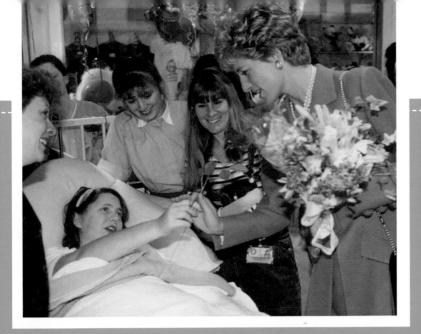

Patient Katie Thomas hands Diana, Princess of Wales a rose on Valentine's Day, the anniversary of the foundation of the hospital

The new building opened in 1875 had wards named after a number of Victoria's children. The *London Journal* reported at the time that. 'the Victoria Ward, the Alexandra Ward, and all the wards named after the Princesses of England – not one of whom is unfamiliar to hospital work – are built of brick, the glazed surface of which is turned within, so that the utmost cleanliness and the most absolute freedom from danger with regard to infectious disease are assured.' As this article implies, many of Victoria's children were active on behalf of the hospital. In 1872, for example, the Prince and Princess of Wales, Edward and Alexandra, laid the foundation stone for the 1875 building.

After the First World War Princess Mary, later the Princess Royal, trained to be a nurse at Great Ormond Street Hospital. She remained a lifelong supporter, as vice-patron and then president until 1948, when the role of president was abolished. She reverted to being vice-patron, which she remained until her death in 1965. In 1963, the Princess opened the Barrie Wing at the hospital.

The Queen first visited the hospital in her coronation year, 1952. She has since visited on both her Silver and Golden Jubilees, when the hospital was celebrating its 125th and 150th anniversaries respectively. In 1986 Charles and Diana, the Prince and Princess of Wales, became the patrons of the highly successful Wishing Well Appeal. In 1989 the formerly abandoned role of president was revived for Princess Diana, a role she held until her death in 1997. Diana was well known for supporting a number of children's charities, and her involvement with Great Ormond Street Hospital was considerable. Her final official visit in the year of her death was to open a new renal unit. The Prince of Wales has continued to be a good friend to Great Ormond Street Hospital, and in 2006 he and the Duchess of Cornwall paid a visit to the newly opened Octav Botnar Wing.

The royal family's support of Great Ormond Street Hospital has now spanned three centuries, and it seems certain to remain a strong feature of the hospital.

SPECIAL APPEAL ON BEHALF OF THE
BUILDING FUND.

THE HOSPITAL FOR SICK CHILDREN,

48 & 49, GREAT ORMOND STREET, LONDON.

Instituted 1852.

The Objects of the Institution are:—

I.—THE MEDICAL AND SURGICAL TREATMENT OF POOR CHILDREN.
II.—THE ATTAINMENT AND DIFFUSION OF KNOWLEDGE REGARDING THE DISEASES OF CHILDREN.
III.—THE TRAINING OF NURSES FOR CHILDREN.

THE WEST FRONT—*Designed by* Mr. EDWARD M. BARRY, R.A.

Every information will be afforded by the Secretary, Mr. SAMUEL WHITFORD, at the Hospital, 49, Great Ormond Street, Bloomsbury, to whom Drafts or Post Office Orders may be made payable.

CONTRIBUTIONS TOWARDS THE NEW BUILDING ARE VERY EARNESTLY SOLICITED.

Bankers.

MESSRS. WILLIAMS, DEACON & Co., 20, Birchin Lane.
MESSRS. HOARE, Fleet Street.
MESSRS. HERRIES, FARQUHAR & Co., St. James' Street.

This appeal for funds to build the first purpose-built hospital building at Great Ormond Street was the first of many campaigns to pay for new construction

In particular, because of the enormous costs involved, charitable income is today required for the redevelopment of the hospital buildings, if they are to meet the exacting standards necessary for the delivery and development of globally pioneering treatments.

Funding new buildings

Money has always been needed for redevelopment. It was the proceeds from the first annual dinner, in 1858, that allowed the purchase of the neighbouring house, 48 Great Ormond Street. After successful appeals, first for the 1875 building and then for the 1893 south wing, there was still a need for a new outpatients building. This was provided in 1908, and called the Astor building after the family that donated the money for its construction.

The drive towards modernisation of the hospital buildings received a big boost in 1929 with the gift of the copyright of *Peter Pan* from JM Barrie. This gift has had a positive impact on the hospital's finances ever since, not only in terms of direct revenue, but also from associated fundraising activities. In 1937, for example, a 'Peter Pan Party' hosted by the Lord

Wishing Well Appeal

By the 1980s the 1875 building could clearly no longer provide adequate quality space for patients and staff. To fund a major redevelopment, the Wishing Well Appeal was launched in 1986 with patronage from the Prince and Princess of Wales. The late Jules Kosky, honorary archivist at the hospital and author in 1991 of a book on its history, wrote, 'What happened was one of the most wonderful things in the history of Great Ormond Street.' Over a period of two years the appeal raised £54 million. This funded the Variety Club Building, which opened in 1994. The Wishing Well Appeal

Mayor of London at the Mansion House raised £60,000 for the rebuilding fund. The building that was partly financed from the proceeds of this evening was opened by King George VI in 1938. In 1946 it became known as the Southwood Building, after the hospital's chairman of 1939–46, Lord Southwood.

Lord Southwood is a key figure in the history of fundraising at the hospital. Using his business acumen acquired as a major newspaper proprietor, he brought approximately £1.5 million to the hospital in one of the most challenging periods in its history. Writing in 1962, sixteen years after Southwood's death, the chairman of the building committee, James Crooks, paid homage to this achievement: 'So we have been able to progress,' he said, 'during the difficult years since the war, because of the money which Lord Southwood collected for us.'

The old 'wishing well' fountain in the garden of the 1875 building from a picture taken in c. 1905

The Garfield Weston Foundation

The Garfield Weston Foundation, the trustees of which are all members of the Weston family, has been a steadfast supporter of the hospital and its work for more than 20 years. Having donated more than £9 million to the hospital the foundation is one of its most generous friends and has enabled it to take some giant steps forward in providing crucial technology and facilities for patients and their parents.

The Garfield Weston Foundation was established in 1958 by Willard Garfield Weston, a Canadian businessman who arrived in the UK with his family in 1932 and was the founder of Associated British Foods. He also established the family's longstanding tradition of active philanthropy across many different areas of society including the arts, education, health and the environment. Chairmanship of the foundation was taken over by his son, known as Garry Weston, through whom the family's philanthropic tradition continued and has carried on doing so since his death in 2002 with Garry's son, Guy, now at the helm.

Great Ormond Street Hospital received its first donation from the foundation in 1987, when it contributed £3 million to the Wishing Well Appeal. The following year it contributed a further £1 million, which meant that the foundation ultimately donated £4 million of the total £54 million raised by the appeal. The money was raised in order to fund a major redevelopment that was desperately needed to replace the decrepit 1875 building. The Variety Club Building which opened in 1994 was its replacement, financed by the proceeds from the Wishing Well Appeal.

Garry Weston's daughter, Sophia Mason and her husband Charles, made a donation towards lifesaving ECMO (Extra Corporeal Membrane Oxygenation) equipment at Great Ormond Street Hospital after their son, Sam, was born with lung failure in August 2000 and

Sam Mason, who was treated at Great Ormond Street Hospital, with Princess Alexandra (left) and his grandmother, Mary Weston, at the opening of Weston House in 2004

was successfully treated at the hospital. In 2006 Charles and Sophia, and, separately, the Foundation, also became members of the hospital's Tick Tock Club which is raising money for the construction of a world-class Heart and Lung Centre.

Perhaps the most recognisable sign of the Garfield Weston Foundation's support for the hospital, though, has been the donation of £5 million for the construction of Weston House. This building, which sits on Great Ormond Street, houses both the Paul O'Gorman Patient Hotel, providing 30 rooms for patient and family accommodation and eight transitional care flats, as well as a staff education and training centre. Moving care out of the institutionalised setting of the hospital and into a more family-friendly surrounding is an important development in modern paediatric care at Great Ormond Street Hospital. The money from the foundation has had a major impact in providing the facilities to accommodate more parents so they can be close to their children, and in improving the environment for children who require longer-term stays.

It is clear that the foundation has had a vast and tangible influence on delivering better quality care at the hospital. For the hospital to continue to remain at the forefront of childhood medicine, it will carry on seeking charitable support and trying to gain similarly generous gifts from other philanthropists. By doing so it can carry on delivering care in better buildings with modern technology, and ultimately more effective outcomes in making children well again in a caring environment.

was named after the fountain that used to stand in the hospital garden, where patients would, it is said, throw coins into the water and wish to get better. It was perhaps the appeal's connection with water which led to the creation of its distinctive teardrop logo, which is still the emblem of the hospital charity more than twenty years later.

A great variety of initiatives

Modern fundraising at the hospital uses a wide variety of techniques to raise money. Furthermore, members of the public independently organise their own fundraising events, and are sponsored for all kinds of activities, from running in marathons to undertaking the Three Peaks Challenge (climbing the highest mountains of England, Scotland and Wales in twenty-four hours), and from riding on horseback from Land's End to John O'Groats to jumping out of aeroplanes.

Treks organised by the charity have taken place in a number of locations, such as The Great Wall of China

as endoscopy and treatments such as enzyme replacement therapy. Staff can see their fundraising efforts reflected in positive developments at the hospital. The money raised is used to fund resources ranging from MRI scanners to a new cardiac operating theatre.

Trekking

The 'challenges department' at Great Ormond Street Hospital Charity organises treks all over the world, from the Inca trail in Peru, to the Great Wall of China, and climbing Mount Kilimanjaro in Tanzania. Approximately 300 members of the public participate in these treks every year. They often have a truly amazing adventure while also raising money for the hospital – £374,000 in 2006. One member of the hospital staff is a particularly keen trekker, having been on the Inca, China, and Namibia treks. She is Zoe Wilks, a modern matron on Kingfisher Ward, a day-care ward which tries to exert the minimum impact on the lives of children undergoing investigations such

British Grand Prix

In addition to enterprising members of staff, many current and former patients have played an enormous part in fundraising efforts, none more so than Kirsteen Lupton. Kirsteen has raised a huge sum of money for Great Ormond Street Hospital, and has spoken at a number of events, including a Formula 1 ball in 2004. Grand Prix Formula 1 teams McLaren and Ferrari have both been involved with the cardiac team at the hospital, passing on their expertise in communication in pressurised situations, as related in Chapter 4. The Formula 1 party, which takes place in association with Great Ormond Street Hospital Charity in the run-up to the British Grand Prix at Silverstone, has become a

Kirsteen Lupton

Kirsteen has not had an ordinary childhood. She auctioned her autograph for £20,000, is the winner of the 2006 Pride of Britain fundraiser of the year award, and has met numerous celebrities and politicians, including Tony Blair. She has also helped to raise more than £800,000 for Great Ormond Street Hospital. Kirsteen has had to overcome serious illness in order to achieve what she has.

Kirsteen was born in Glasgow in 1993 with her bladder outside her body (known as bladder exstrophy), a condition that affects approximately one in every 40,000 babies, Kirsteen required surgery the day she was born, enduring an operation that lasted five hours.

Kirsteen's operation was the first of many at a Glasgow hospital, which culminated in something called a 'Mitrofanoff procedure'. This is an operation that allows the patient to empty their bladder through a tube (catheter) in their abdomen about once every four hours, without worrying about incontinence. However, the surgery did not go well and Kirsteen was referred to Great Ormond Street Hospital in 1999, under the care of consultant urologist Phillip Ransley. In September 2000, Kirsteen underwent major surgery that was made more complicated by the previously unsuccessful intervention. As a result, just a fortnight after the operation she required further emergency surgery.

Kirsteen's dad, Martin, says that 'it was undoubtedly the worst experience of our lives... Kirsteen was screaming "save me, save me" as she was pushed along the corridor. I remember seeing the two nurses that had come down to the theatre with us collapsing in tears.'

However, the operation was successful and Kirsteen was able to leave the hospital soon after. She says that 'before my surgery I was very limited in what I was able to do... I can now live my life in a way that my family and I could once only dream of.'

Kirsteen has since helped the hospital enormously through her fundraising work for the hospital charity. She has made numerous appearances and speeches at many events, including the Silverstone Grand Prix Ball.

'It is a real honour to speak at events on behalf of the hospital,' she says. 'I would do absolutely anything to support Great Ormond Street Hospital because they've helped me so much.'

Kirsteen with actor Jude Law and her Pride of Britain award in 2006

The Harris family

Lord and Lady Harris have been supporters of Great Ormond Street Hospital since the late 1980s, but a major donation in 2005 to help build the Harris International Patient Centre in the hospital's new Octav Botnar Wing was largely inspired by their son and daughter-in-law witnessing first-hand some of the terrible consequences of the Asian tsunami of 2004.

Lord and Lady Harris with their son and daughter-in-law Martin and Zoe Harris

Lord Harris of Peckham is one of the UK's leading businessmen, the founder of the chain of Carpetright stores. Lord and Lady Harris are also among the country's leading philanthropists, and have donated over £100 million to a number of good causes, including Great Ormond Street Hospital.

The Harris family have made an enormous contribution to the care of children at Great Ormond Street Hospital. Their support began during the Wishing Well Appeal in the late 1980s, with a gift towards the construction of the Variety Club Building. They have also funded pioneering equipment – a dual-headed SPECT-CT imaging camera. This provides three-dimensional images of blood flow, aiding in the early diagnosis, treatment and prevention of childhood cancers.

More recently, Lord Harris and his family have helped to support the first phase of the hospital's redevelopment programme. On holiday in Thailand on 26 December 2004, Martin and Zoe saw the devastation and loss of life caused by the tsunami, and wanted to make a donation to healthcare which would benefit children from around the world. The subsequent major gift to Great Ormond Street Hospital, from the Harris family, helped to finance the Harris International Patient Centre which opened in 2006.

This new centre provides care for overseas children who do not have access to the expert and specialised treatments available at Great Ormond Street Hospital. Often their care is paid for by their governments, who cannot provide the treatment in their own countries. The Harris International Patient Centre is located over three floors of the Octav Botnar Wing, and houses inpatient and outpatient facilities as well as two operating theatres.

This generous gift has made an enormous difference to the lives of many children from around the world. Not only do they receive excellent medical treatment, but the children also benefit from the being cared for in an extremely modern, well-designed and welcoming environment.

One of the many 'fairies' at the charity event – 'Peter Pan in Kensington Gardens'

major fixture in the hospital charity's calendar and has raised large amounts of money – £150,000 in one night in 2006, for example. The connection has also allowed many patients from the hospital to attend the British Grand Prix at Silverstone, meet the drivers and even sit in the racing cars!

Peter Pan

Another major annual event of recent years, organised by the charity, has been 'Peter Pan in Kensington Gardens', a day of family fun and activities in the very place where Barrie is said to have found inspiration for

Peter Pan. This event, which has such an integral link with the hospital's history, is another opportunity for many patients at the hospital to have a fun day out as well as celebrating Barrie's important legacy to the hospital.

Peter Pan has also been the inspiration for many 'Peter Pan Days' in schools across the country, in which children dress up and play

Hillingdon primary school at their Peter Pan Day in 2006

CHILDREN with CANCER UK

The stated aim of the charity CHILDREN with CANCER UK (until recently called CHILDREN with LEUKAEMIA UK) has never pulled any punches – it has always been to 'conquer childhood cancer'. The charity states that, 'it wants all children diagnosed with cancer to be cured, and for the cure to be effected with minimum disruption to their lives.' The charity and its aims were born out of a cruel double tragedy for its founders, Eddie and Marion O'Gorman.

Eddie O'Gorman, chairman of CHILDREN with CANCER UK, wants to help make childhood cancer deaths a thing of the past. His son, Paul, was diagnosed with leukaemia – a cancer of the blood – aged fourteen; he died just three months later, in February 1987. Before he died, Paul had made his parents promise to help other children with the disease, and in November that year Eddie and his wife Marion held their first fundraising ball. Paul's sister, Jean, attended the ball in a wheelchair and wearing an oxygen mask, as she was also extremely unwell. She was critically ill with cancer, and died just two days later. Shortly afterwards, Eddie and Marion met Diana, Princess of Wales, who at the time was patron with Prince Charles of Great Ormond Street Hospital's Wishing Well Appeal. She was deeply moved by the O'Gormans' double tragedy, and offered her personal assistance in founding the charity which she inaugurated in January 1988. It has ever since been based on Great Ormond Street, opposite the hospital.

Eddie O'Gorman with his wife, Marion, and daughter Sandra outside the Paul O'Gorman Patient Building at Great Ormond Street Hospital

'It's impossible to get over losing two children,' says Eddie, 'but instead of giving up and hiding, Marion and I stood up to the problem and have raised more than £80 million to try to do something about leukaemia.'

As the largest centre in the UK for childhood leukaemia and other cancers, treating one in every ten children diagnosed with cancer in the country, Great Ormond Street Hospital would inevitably have a close link with the charity, and it has benefited enormously from the money raised. Since 1988, the hospital has received more than £12 million from CHILDREN with CANCER UK. This money has been spent on several major initiatives, including a cancer research centre, a patient hotel in Weston House – called the Paul O'Gorman Patient Hotel, and a redevelopment of the hospital's oncology and haematology facilities, as well as many individual research projects.

'Cancer is not going away,' says Eddie, 'and we need to carry on funding research, treatment and welfare of the children who have cancer. With the research we're giving more of a chance to future generations – finding out the causes of cancer and discovering new treatments. Great Ormond Street Hospital has the expertise, and it is easy to give money to it – we know that the money we're giving is being used for the best possible cause.'

while raising money for the hospital. In many cases, the pupils masquerading as Peter, Tinker Bell or the pirates are classmates of a patient at the hospital, inspired to raise money by seeing the plight of their friend.

City trading days

A spectacular fundraising success for the hospital has been an annual trading day, in which major banks in the City of London participate in a 'mock trade'. Donations are gathered from the bank's employees and clients, and matched by corporate giving. In December 2006, for example, staff at Citigroup (Fixed Income), J. P. Morgan, and Macquarie banks raised an astonishing £600,000 during an adrenaline-charged trading challenge. That sum was enough to pay for twenty-seven vital bedside monitors in the Intensive Care Unit. The event showed what can be achieved in a very short space of time, and what a huge impact such money can have. This event, like so many others, was supported by a number of celebrities, all of whom have been absolutely critical to many of the hospital charity's fundraising successes.

Great Ormond Street Hospital for Children
NHS Trust

Great Ormond Street Hospital's major supporters

Great Ormond Street Hospital has been very fortunate to receive wonderfully generous support from many people since it was first established in 1852. We have always relied on the generosity of our supporters to continue to provide the very best medical care for sick children in the UK, and indeed from around the world.

I am extremely grateful to every single person who has helped the hospital, but would like to make particular reference to the extremely generous group of individuals and charitable trusts who have made the truly remarkable gesture of giving £1,000,000 or more. These exceptional gifts have truly helped shape the hospital and allowed it to become one of the most important children's hospitals in the world. Amongst this group I am delighted to acknowledge the following:

Action Medical Research, The David & Frederick Barclay Foundation, The Botnar family, British Heart Foundation, The Bunting family, CHILDREN with CANCER UK, The Djanogly Foundation, The Clore Duffield Foundation, The Philip and Pauline Harris Charitable Trust, Liechtenstein Global Trust, Oak Foundation, Reuben Foundation, Mrs Phyllis Somers, Hugh and Catherine Stevenson, Sir Alan Sugar, The Bernard Sunley Charitable Foundation, The Philip Ullmann Trust, The Variety Club Children's Charity, The Garfield Weston Foundation, The Wolfson Foundation, The Charles Wolfson Charitable Trust

Jane Collins

Dr Jane Collins
Chief Executive

Major donors

Trusts, foundations, philanthropic individuals and even other charities wanting to finance research, treatment and equipment are all major donors to the hospital.

This is just a sample of the range of endeavour involved in successfully raising millions of pounds for Great Ormond Street Hospital every year. *Charity is still an essential part of the funding of the hospital*, and it must remain so if the hospital is to retain its historically pioneering trajectory and its current world-class status, to give the most seriously ill children the best possible treatment.

Businesses

Thousands of companies, from local businesses to internationally recognised brands, have supported the hospital throughout its long history. Listed here are just a few of

the companies that have made a significant impact in recent years:

BT IP Networking, Citigroup, Deutsche Bank, Estée Lauder, Formula One Management, Goldman Sachs, HSBC, JP Morgan, Macquarie, Mapeley, Pirates Adventures, Morgan Stanley, The Walt Disney Company.

The Tick Tock Club

Launched in May 2006 under the leadership of patron Gary Lineker and chairman Ken Costa, the Tick Tock Club – a unique charitable members' club – is raising funds to help build a new heart and lung centre. We would like to thank the following members for their generous support:

Terry Adams, Nick and Kate Austin, Mr Tony Ball, Mr and Mrs Peter Beckwith, Alan and Sara Bennie, Emily and Len Blavatnik, Tim and Sarah Bunting, John and Susan Burns, Standard Chartered Plc, Sir Trevor and Lady Chinn, Mr and Mrs Ken Costa, Doctor Genevieve and Mr Peter Davies, Ian and Penny Davis , Sarah and Lloyd Dorfman, Mr and Mrs Alex Easton, AAC Group Ltd, Michael and Francesca Evans, Dorotheé and Pierre-Henri Flamand, Jacob and Verette Schimmel, Charles and Kaaren Hale, Alan and Christiane Hodson, C. T. Van Hoorn Charitable Trust, Vivid Imaginations, David and Elizabeth James, The Jenkins Family, The Juice Group Limited, Rose Marie and Erland Karlsson, Keith and Muriel Lipman, Gavin and Luise MacDonald, Charles and Sophia Mason, Scott and Suling Mead, The Maaike McInnes Charitable Trust, George Michael and Kenny Goss, Mitch and Alison Moore, Andrew and Marina Newington, Amicia and Richard Oldfield, Elizabeth and Daniel Peltz Simon Picken QC and Dr Sophie Picken, Paul and Deidre Pindar, The Reuben Foundation, Stuart and Bianca Roden, Lady Rothes, The Dr Mortimer and Theresa Sackler Foundation, The Basil Samuel Charitable Foundation, Vipin and Beatrice Sareen, Ian and Carol Sellars, The Michael Shanly Charitable Trust, Dominic and Cathy Shorthouse, Hugh and Catherine Stevenson, Sir Alan and Lady Sugar, Andrew and Katrina Taee, The Taylor Family Foundation, The Thornton Foundation, Stanley and Beatrice Tollman, Toy Trust, Michael and Rachel Weston, The Garfield Weston Foundation, Mr Pierre and Dr Yvonne Winkler, Mr and Mrs Roger Wyatt and those who wish to remain anonymous.

Winner of the 13-and-over patient competition category, Harriet Fulcher tells her story.

13-and-over winner: Harriet Fulcher

How GOSH Changed My Life
By Harriet Fulcher

Chocolate, Jokes, Friends, Catherine Tate, Family, Pets and a cosy bed.

Do all these things make you smile? Imagine for a moment if you couldn't.

In June 2004 I was told I may never smile again, after six months I could, This is my story.

June the 7th 2004, back to school after an exciting half term break, Couldn't wait to see everybody. 3 o'clock schools ended and back at home, going to meet my friends at the park, as it's a hot summer's day, my best friend Lilly's knocking for me soon, can't wait to show her my dress from being bridesmaid for my auntie and uncle the previous weekend. 4 o' clock now heading towards the park, we meet some other friends heading our way, Woops, Joe drops this weird shape ring he found, I step forward to pick it up...

I've just been hit by a car...

Everything's a blur, I'm bleeding through my ears and nose, my shoulder hurts, I'm in pain, there's blood on the road people all around me, they sort me out, an ambulance is here, they strap me up and place me inside, all I can hear is mum; don't shut your eyes, keep your eyes open. I arrive at the Southend hospital, they put my into an induced coma to stabilise me to keep my air wave open, they scanned me due to my head injury and told my mum and dad I was being sent to Great Ormond Street Hospital because of my dreadful injuries.

I've arrived at Great Ormond Street, I've been admitted to PICU (paediatric intensive care unit) ward, I'm still in an induced coma, After 14 hours I've now woken up, is this just a dream, I don't remember what happened, my mum explains to me that I've been in a tragic car accident, the doctors are asking me what is the date, I reply the 7th of June 2004, I was a day behind, I didn't realise the extent of my injuries which were, broken collar bone, minor cuts and bruises, contusion to my left lung, a partially severed ear, perforated ear drum and a skull fracture. I'm still heavily sedated; my ear has been repaired with plastic surgery.

Im starting to come out of my coma, mum and dad are now starting to notice something different, the left hand side of my face is still and lopsided, Doctors examined the problem and consulted a specialist from the nearby Royal National ENT (Ear Nose and Throat) Hospital. I've just be told that I urgently needed surgery to release the pressure on my nerves from my skull fracture. Six and a half hours of neurosurgery later I'm being put into high dependency ward to recover. 12th of June, my head is in incredible pain and is bandaged up, and I'm back at Great Ormond Street.

Mum helps me out of bed, I'm now seeing my self for the first time since my accident, I'm speechless, my eyes are filling up, I've turned to mum in tears, Thinking how awful I look.

I've lost my smile...

The doctors are now telling me, it could take a year to eighteen months for my face to recover, they then said, but we cannot guarantee a full recovery. I also faced hundreds of hours of intensive Physiotherapy for my facial paralysis.

The Doctors are doing more tests on me as my hearing in my left ear is not quite right, the skull fracture has caused damage to my inner ear with a permanent 35% loss of hearing.

It has now been three years since being at GOSH, I have made a remarkable recovery, after returning to school just 4 months after my accident. I briefly remember my accident, and some of my first few days in hospital, but I have not forgotten the support that my family, close friends and care I received at GOSH.

Since I've returned from Great Ormond Street, I have appeared on TV and spoken at events for GOSH talking about my experience and recovery and the care I received at GOSH.

My family and I have held fundraising events each year since my accident in aid of GOSH and raised over £21,000 so far with more to come in the future. But this could never repay them, for what they have done for me and my smile.

Chapter 8

Buildings

'We shape our buildings; thereafter they shape us.'
Winston Churchill

Great Ormond Street Hospital's buildings have always played an important part in its story. Not only have they provided the physical structures essential for the delivery of the hospital's treatments and care, they have also been a temporary home for millions of children, the doughty survivors of bombs, and the subject of enormous debate, drama and toil. This chapter tells the story of some of those buildings, and looks at how architecture, art and design are being used at the hospital today to create a friendly and effective healing environment for its patients. If Churchill was right in saying that buildings exert a dramatic influence on the people who use them, then special attention must surely be paid to buildings for children, who are so sensitive to their environment.

Art in modern buildings, such as this piece by Kenny Hunter in the Octav Botnar Wing, is used to create an environment in which children can feel comfortable

A healing environment

Increasingly today, it is recognised that architecture can play an integral role in the healing process, by creating environments where children feel as comfortable and happy as possible. But creating a sympathetic place where children could be treated was also a concern of the founders of the hospital. This may seem surprising, as the old Victorian blocks built by the generation that founded Great Ormond Street continue to be demolished around the country. Cold, austere, high-ceilinged brick buildings, with long corridors and enormous open wards, are certainly not regarded today as the ideal environment for sick children. But the children who came to Great Ormond Street Hospital in the 19th century were often from poverty-stricken, squalid homes. At the hospital, by contrast, they found order and cleanliness.

A refuge near its patients

The Hospital for Sick Children, before it even found its home on Great Ormond Street, had identified its patient base as being among the poor. It was therefore important for it to be located near where these people lived. When the first major expansion of the hospital was being planned, in 1869, it was suggested that the hospital move to open land that had yet to be built upon, probably in west London. Dr Charles West, for one, was against the idea of moving. 'It is essential, if the hospital is to receive cases of acute disease,' he said, 'that it should not be too far removed from the dwellings of the poor.' At Great Ormond Street some of the most notorious slums of London were close by, from Seven Dials in the west to Saffron Hill in the east. It was this very proximity to poverty which contributed to the fact observed by West that, 'The very large proportion, at least 80 per cent, of the patients of the hospital come from within a distance of two miles; many from within a mile of the institution.'

Away from the bustle

But although the new hospital was very close to the centre of London, it avoided the busy thoroughfares. Great Ormond Street had, in the 18th century, been extremely fashionable, but by the 1850s it had become a backwater. *Fraser's Magazine* applauded the hospital's location in an article written in 1855. 'In selecting Great Ormond

The original townhouse at 49 Great Ormond Street, containing a single ward, was the first home of the hospital from 1852

Street as the situation for the hospital, the committee have certainly been successful in satisfying the first condition required of them – a retired situation. Great Ormond Street is a street of the past – an air of dreamy solitude, of mysterious desolation hangs about it, that makes you feel far indeed removed from the busy haunts of men.' An article from the *Observer* in 1859 emphasised the tranquillity of Great Ormond Street still further, when it said that 'grass grows in the broad street'. Perhaps less encouragingly for the site of a hospital, the article in *Fraser's Magazine* goes on to say that, 'The antiquated mansions have a spectral aspect; they look like a city of the dead; a sort of cockney Pompeii restored to the light of day after a trance of centuries.' However, it seems the writer saw the hospital's late 17th-century townhouse as some kind of beacon amidst the gloom: 'Standing out from among these dwellings of our forefathers, with a fresh white stuccoed front, which gives to it an air of comparative juvenility suited to its destination, is No. 49, the Hospital we have to visit.'

Starting out small was a deliberate intention of the founders of the hospital, in Britain a children's hospital was an untried experiment, so it was seen as prudent not to be too ambitious. Dr Mead's Queen Anne townhouse, with its wood panelled walls, spacious library and garden for the recovering patients was seen as an ideal choice. (Indeed Charles Dickens had written, in *Drooping Buds*, 'a garden and playground for the convalescent is an essential requisite'.) It met the approval of the *London Journal* in an article from 1858: 'As they lie in bed, their wistful eyes gaze on no white-washed wall or smoke-and-dust-bestained ceiling. No: the ceiling is absolutely rich in mouldings and gilding, and the walls are crowded with coloured prints.' It quickly became apparent, however, that the demand for the hospital was far greater than the original facilities could provide, and in the same year as this article, 1858, the neighbouring property was purchased. This increased the number of inpatient beds from twenty to seventy-five. Nevertheless, within a decade the hospital was under pressure to expand again.

Expansion plans

Discussions began in 1869 as to exactly what form that expansion should take. Dr Charles West was at the heart of these debates, and counselled in favour of caution in terms of both the size and the location of the expansion. 'The idea of establishing a large hospital such as should rival in size the general hospitals of the metropolis [containing more than 300 beds] is very tempting,' he said, 'but I apprehend by no means possible.' West favoured a hospital of about 150 beds, and although he was in principle not against a move from Great Ormond Street, he was reluctant to move very far. 'Now if a site could be found within the limits of our means, and also within reach of the poor, sufficiently large to furnish a garden for the children, and in an open situation, there can I think be no doubt that it would be most desirable to secure it.' No such site could be found nearby, however. It was therefore decided to build the new hospital in the gardens of numbers 48 and 49 Great Ormond Street, hence its nickname, 'The Hospital in the Garden'.

'The Hospital in the Garden'

The architect chosen to design the new hospital was Edward Middleton Barry, son of Sir Charles Barry who, with Augustus Pugin, had designed the Houses of Parliament. After his father's death in 1860, Edward took on the supervision of works on the Houses of Parliament, before he turned his attention to the Great Ormond Street Hospital project at the beginning of the 1870s. Thus began a close link between the Barry family (no relation to JM Barrie) and the hospital, that saw Edward design the 1875 building and chapel, his brother Alfred perform the opening service at the chapel, and his other brother Charles design the 1893 south wing and the 1908 Astor outpatients building.

In 1872, when the 1875 building was still in its early stages, the forerunner of the *Architects' Journal*, *The Builder*, gave an insight into some of the major considerations instrumental in its design:

THE HOSPITAL FOR SICK CHILDREN,
49, GREAT ORMOND STREET.

Patron—HER MAJESTY THE QUEEN.
Vice Patrons { H.R.H. THE PRINCESS OF WALES.
{ H.R.H. THE PRINCESS CHRISTIAN.

PROGRAMME
OF THE
Ceremony of laying the Foundation Stone
OF THE
NEW BUILDING, GREAT ORMOND STREET,
BY
HER ROYAL HIGHNESS
THE PRINCESS OF WALES,
On THURSDAY, JULY 11, 1872,
At Half-past Three o'Clock.

The programme for the laying of the foundation stone of the 1875 hospital building. The ceremony was 'repeated' more than a hundred years later when Diana, Princess of Wales did the same thing for the 1994 Variety Club Building

The 'ceremony of laying the foundation stone' in 1872

children's own clothes can be kept, in order to secure neatness and order.

In connexion with the wards themselves, in addition to the bathroom and water-closets which are needed in all hospitals alike, it is very important to provide a ward kitchen, where milk, beef tea, and the various little articles of food so much needed for children can be kept in readiness day and night, without the necessity of sending it to the kitchen. It is also necessary to provide a vestiary in connection with each ward, in which not only the Ward linen, but also the

The result of three years of construction by contractors Messrs Perry was a new 100-bed, state-of-the-art hospital. It had six large wards, a purpose-built operating theatre, a substantial outpatients department in the basement, and even a sophisticated underfloor heating system. The annual report for 1875 was proud to extol the virtues of the hospital's new building: 'On the 19th of November last [the hospital] threw open the doors of a new building, furnished with every modern appliance, for the alleviation of infantile diseases and sufferings.'

The 1875 hospital building. On the far right of the picture is the original hospital at number 49 before it was knocked down and replaced by the south wing, now called the Paul O'Gorman building

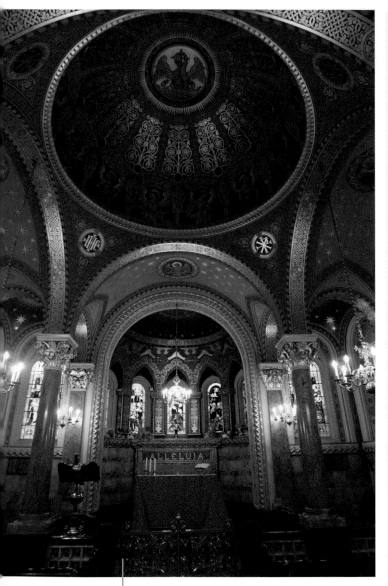

The hospital chapel is not only a notable architectural feature and a beautiful space, it has also been an important place for families with extreme emotions to be able to sit and contemplate

The chapel

The high-Victorian, neo-Gothic-red-brick hospital was perhaps not the most eye-catching of buildings, though it clearly had an air of solidity, even grandeur, about it, but it was built primarily for practicality, order and cleanliness. It also included, however, a sparkling architectural gem in the form of the chapel, which has survived long after the rest of the building was demolished. Oscar Wilde, for one, thought the chapel a splendid thing:

> For my part, having visited the hospital on more than one occasion, I have seen that high kind of beauty which consists in the absence of useless ornaments, and also that more spiritual beauty that any visitor can see who chooses to enter the chapel of the hospital, which I consider to be one of the most beautiful private chapels that we have in any hospital in London.

Although small, the chapel is elaborately decorated in a Byzantine style. The *London Journal* described the interior décor on the occasion of the opening of the building in

Moving the chapel in its entirety so that it could fit in with the new buildings in the 1990s was an enormous challenge. The building is seen here encased and moving along its 'rails'

November 1875: 'The walls are lined with alabaster, the columns and pilasters are of rare Devonshire marble, and the whole is decorated in gold and colour of the most elaborate description.' The newspaper was pleased, though, that the hospital's own money had not been spent on such an ornate interior, and gave its approval to the more austere decoration used in the rest of the building: 'The decorations... are as inexpensive... they are nevertheless as bright and cheerful and pleasant to the eyes of children and men as any decorations of their kind.'

The chapel was actually endowed by a private individual, who at the time of the building's opening remained anonymous. But it seems the identity of the benefactor completes the Barry circle, as it was the architect's cousin, William Darry. This means that three different members of the Barry family respectively paid for, designed and blessed the chapel.

When it was finally decided, more than a hundred years later, that the 1875 building was no longer capable of serving the needs of the hospital, the demolition programme spared the chapel. For almost 120 years it had been a place where people would go with the strongest emotions of all kinds – hope, despair, joy and sorrow – and it was this, as well as the architectural merit of the building, that allowed it to be saved. There was a catch, however: in order to survive, and to accommodate the new Variety Club Building, the chapel had to be moved. This was not an easy task, even for a very small building. A concrete cast was laid underneath it and the building was supported by jacks. The whole chapel was then placed in a giant box and moved by sliding it along a track with hydraulic ram-jacks into its new position. The move itself in 1990 took just two days, but it was the result of several years' preparation.

The convalescent homes

In 1869 Great Ormond Street Hospital opened its first convalescent home at Cromwell House, a 17th-century house in Highgate. When Highgate became well and truly an integral part of London, Cromwell House was no longer deemed a suitable location for convalescing children. From 1927 patients were instead sent to Tadworth Court in Surrey, particularly children suffering from orthopaedic and rheumatic conditions.

New demands

The increasing number of patients, and the new facilities required such as pathology labs and an X-ray department, necessitated further growth in the capacity of the hospital's buildings as it moved into the 20th century. The 1893 building, designed by Charles Barry, helped to fulfil the hospital's evolving needs and still stands today. It features deep but patched-up scars from shrapnel caused by bombs dropped during the Blitz. It is now named the Paul O'Gorman building, after a fourteen-year-old boy who died of leukaemia in 1987. His parents, Eddie and Marion O'Gorman, set up the charity CHILDREN with LEUKAEMIA UK (now known as CHILDREN with CANCER UK), which has been one of Great Ormond Street Hospital's most generous supporters.

In 1891 it was still uncertain whether the new building would actually be built, because funds were so short. In January 1892 there was a desperate appeal for further funding from the management committee: 'In order to complete and furnish the Wing, the Committee estimate that a further sum of not less than Twelve Thousand Pounds will be required; and they

The 1875 building on the left with its distinctive towers was actually on Powis Place; the south wing of the building opened in 1893 faces onto Great Ormond Street and is the only building pictured which still stands today

appeal earnestly to the Governors and to the Public generally for this sum.' The money was found, and the committee was happy to report the following year that the building was now ready for occupation. This same need for charitable funds for redevelopment is a feature of modern efforts towards building a better future for the hospital.

The Astor building

A new outpatients building was urgently needed in the early years of the 20th century, to cope with approximately 70,000 outpatient visits a year. This project did not cause the committee such financial worries, thanks to the generosity of the American newspaper proprietor, Waldorf Astor. He made a donation to the hospital in memory of his late daughter, Gwendolyn Enid Astor. Photographs of the 1908 Astor Building, which was demolished in 1938, show that it was a capacious building – looking more like an aircraft hangar, perhaps, than a hospital department. Stories of the famous surgeon Sir Denis Browne practising his tennis in the building once all the patients had

gone home do not seem beyond the realm of possibility! The annual report for 1908 included a description of the new building, which reveals a highly reasoned approach to its layout:

'The department consists of three halls – in the first the patients are received and sorted; in the second they wait to see the doctors, and thence they pass on to the third, in which they receive medicine at the dispensary. On to these halls open the necessary rooms for consultation, isolation, investigation and two operating theatres. The patients both come in and go out by Great Ormond Street; and when once they have entered the building, they never have to

This picture of the waiting hall in the capacious Astor building shows children and mothers alike dressed in their finest clothes waiting to be seen by doctors. It is likely that many of the women, from extremely poor backgrounds, would have to have borrowed their hats

retrace their steps, so that the mass of children and mothers moves in one direction only, and confusion is avoided.'

Sprawling growth

Dr Poynton recalls in his memoirs that, 'It might have been hoped that then things would be happy, but no! Massage department, electrical department, research departments were pressing, in every direction one saw small buildings or shanties.' His memories, and those of other observers from this period, describe fairly improvised buildings housing various parts of the hospital beyond the better planned central structures. The First World War put a hold on further construction work, and after it the hospital's finances were in a terrible state.

Between the wars

Nevertheless, during the 1920s Great Ormond Street Hospital began to confront its terminal lack of space, first through a project to create a huge countryside home for the hospital called 'The Children's Hospital City', and then, after that scheme had failed and the new

convalescent home had opened at Tadworth in 1927, through the purchase of the grounds of the nearby Foundling Hospital, known as Coram's Fields. The successful purchase of this site would probably have allowed the hospital to develop a large, low-level solution to meet all its demands. But the sale did not go ahead, a decision confirmed in 1929 to Poynton's enormous disappointment and some bitterness. 'How near we got to success I dare not write. Sufficient to say that there must have been some who at all costs were bent on destroying this great scheme. They succeeded.'

This left Great Ormond Street Hospital with the challenge of providing for its needs on a small and congested 'island' site, sandwiched between Guildford Street to the north and Great Ormond Street to the south. This challenge remains today. It has been complicated in recent times by planning restrictions called 'viewing corridors', which protect views from certain points in London by limiting the height of buildings that fall within them, such as Great Ormond Street. This is a significant constraint on a small site, where the obvious solution is to build upwards.

The approach taken in the 1930s was

The Southwood building, officially opened in 1938, offered a relatively high-rise solution on the cramped inner city site after plans to build on nearby Coram's Field fell through in the 1920s

The post-war years

The Astor building was demolished in 1938 to make way for a high-rise outpatients building, but because of the Second World War this was never built. Instead, after the war a lower-level building was erected on Great Ormond Street. The post-war era also saw the construction of a number of other utilitarian buildings, including the Barrie Wing in 1963, and the troubled Cardiac Wing, which finally opened after many delays in 1987.

The Variety Club Building provided a welcome element of modernity when it was opened in 1994. This was funded from the proceeds of the Wishing Well Appeal.

certainly high-rise, for the time. Two major new buildings were built – in 1934 an eight-storey nurses' home on Guildford Street (awarded a prestigious Royal Institute of British Architects (RIBA) gold medal), and in 1938 a ten-storey building, which in 1946 became known as the Southwood Building. This introduced smaller units, allowing more individual space for patients and preventing the spread of infection. It survived direct hits from the bombings of September 1940 and was immediately repaired.

Bomb damage caused by bombs dropped in September 1940

Before the Second World War the hospital was surrounded by terraced 18th-and-19th century houses; after the war, because of the extensive bomb damage, its urban context changed dramatically

A new development programme

Despite these new buildings, it was widely appreciated that further redevelopment was still needed to provide the best possible spaces for modern clinical facilities and new models of care, a genuinely healing environment for patients, and an excellent working space and amenities for staff. This resulted in a long-term, multi-phase redevelopment programme that has already delivered some highly impressive and award-winning buildings. In 2006, for example, Great Ormond Street Hospital won several awards at the *Building Better Healthcare Awards*

for three projects which have delivered significant value to the hospital. These are Weston House, the Octav Botnar Wing and the Orangery.

The Orangery

In declaring it a national winner in 2005, the RIBA described the Orangery as 'a piece of serendipity dropped into the heart of Great Ormond Street Hospital'. RIBA's commendation for the building said, 'This is architecture as therapy and both architect and client deserve equal credit for it.' The Orangery, between the Southwood Building and the Nurses' Home, is

The spectacular Orangery by SPACELABUK at the very heart of the densely developed Great Ormond Street Hospital site

the first phase of the redevelopment with the Octav Botnar Wing and Weston House. Roger Horn was Great Ormond Street Hospital's design champion from 1999 to 2006. In 2006 he said that:

> In appointing architects and all the design team for the first phase of the redevelopment, we sought to raise the design game. Our aim is world-class services in world-class facilities, and we see that design has a crucial role to play in the healing environment. We also strive to be an excellent employer, and improving the working environment for staff is important.

The Octav Botnar Wing

The Octav Botnar Wing is an attractive and well-integrated steel, glass and brick clinical building, designed by Anshen and Allen. It features state-of-the-art facilities, and its spacious layout admits a large amount of natural light, particularly into the patients' rooms. The

an area for eating and drinking for staff, patients and parents, consisting of both an interior space and exterior decking. It was financed by a specific private donation, and designed by SPACELABUK. It has transformed an unpromising and redundant area into an uplifting place for all who use it.

The Orangery demonstrates the high design values in place at Great Ormond Street Hospital as it delivers its vital redevelopment programme. These values were a major consideration when the key appointments were made for supplying

aim, says Horn, was to create 'a calming, friendly and non-institutional feel'. The building accommodates eighty patient beds and two new operating theatres, as well as comprehensive facilities for parents.

But there is another prominent feature of this building – the way in which art has been integrated into its layout. Artworks, including sculptures by Kenny Hunter, an enormous installation by Claire Twomey and colourful digital animations in the lifts by Hoss Gifford, feature prominently in the building. Great Ormond Street Hospital is committed to providing a therapeutic environment in which artwork is a key element, as these three pieces all demonstrate. The hospital's approach reflects a belief in art as hugely significant, not only for way-finding but most importantly to enhance the overall space. The use of art is proven to be beneficial to children's well-being, reducing the clinical look of the hospital which can aid healing. It also helps to create a relaxed, interesting and interactive environment where children can feel more at ease. This is all part of the hospital's outlook – looking beyond clinical outcomes alone to the overall quality of experience for its patients and their families.

The atrium of the Octav Botnar Wing features this spectacular inflatable sculpture, visible from both the wards inside and the street outside

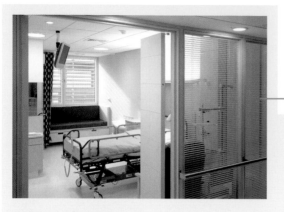

New wards at the hospital have improved facilities for patients and parents alike. There is an emphasis on light and spaciousness

Weston House

This outlook is also reflected in the other key building in phase one of the redevelopment programme, Weston House, which contains the Paul O'Gorman patient hotel. This building provides thirty rooms for parent and family accommodation, as well as eight transitional care flats, and a staff training and education centre. The transitional care flats offer a supportive, home-from-home environment where families can learn to provide long-term care for their children before they return to their home or local hospital. The building, which opened in 2004, delivers enormous benefits for patients, parents and staff alike. It is a valuable example of a non-clinical building giving enormous support to the overall work of the hospital, increasing the flexibility of its care packages, and improving facilities for staff. It has also been a very welcome addition to the streetscape on Great Ormond Street.

Delivery of this phase of the redevelopment programme has been almost entirely paid for (approximately 97 per cent) by charitable donation, which has allowed the hospital to

The spacious entrance to the Octav Botnar Wing is both colourful and dramatic, with ceramic objects ranging from cricket bats to tea cups, projecting from the walls

Phase two

The next stage of the redevelopment, phase two, is being designed by the architects Llewelyn Davies Yeang. It is jointly funded by the NHS and charitable donation. These new buildings are looked at in this book's final chapter, on the future of Great Ormond Street Hospital. Certainly for redevelopment, as for many other aspects of the hospital, charitable income remains absolutely vital if Great Ormond Street Hospital is to continue to improve the health of children by being a global centre of excellence for specialist paediatric services, and for research and education in the field of child health. Future charitable income will enable the hospital to provide the best possible buildings for its patients, their families and its staff. The exciting results from the first phase of the redevelopment suggest that the right team and a powerful vision are in place for the hospital to achieve these aims.

develop such high-quality buildings. As Dr Jane Collins, chief executive of the hospital said, 'At Great Ormond Street Hospital, we hope to invest more in terms of space, flexibility and longevity. We can only do this because financing the development through charitable support gives us the flexibility to do so. Without our donors' generosity we could not deliver this quality.'

Weston House is a non-clinical building which combines the most modern services, yet which sympathetically integrates with the streetscape of Great Ormond Street

Linford Christie, one of the greatest sprinters of his generation, talks about his daughter Briannah's experience of Great Ormond Street.

My daughter, Briannah, had gastroschisis when she was born in 1997. Her bowels were outside her body, and she needed an operation to have them placed back inside. So, at just four hours old, she was taken to Great Ormond Street for treatment. We were really worried and wanted our new baby to be at home, but we also knew that she was in the right place to get the best possible care.

The staff were all extremely compassionate, but at that time, due to the facilities, it was very difficult for more than one parent to stay with Briannah overnight. I was pleased to hear that new developments at Great Ormond Street have made it easier for both parents to be with their child when they are an inpatient at the hospital.

The surgeon and all the staff made us feel comfortable in an extremely trying situation, and we thought the treatment that Briannah received was excellent. Thankfully, it was also successful. Just three weeks after she was admitted, we were able to take our baby home with us. She has been able to grow up fit and healthy, and is living a normal life.

Great Ormond Street Hospital is absolutely the only place I would want my children to go to if they were seriously ill. Without it, Briannah wouldn't be here today.

I have done a number of fundraising events for the hospital, and I cannot thank the staff enough for the brilliant job they did in looking after my daughter.

Linford says that he is extremely grateful to the hospital for giving his daughter such excellent treatment

Linford Christie teams up with other successful athletes, Fatima Whitbread, and Paralympic basketball bronze medallist Ade Adepitan at the 'Sporting Greats' fundraising event for Great Ormond Street Hospital in 2005

Chapter 9

The Future

'The story of The Hospital for Sick Children in Great Ormond Street, like others of its kind, may seem to some of little moment in relation to the sway and surge of great events. Yet in truth it is an epic of achievement in service to a great ideal, pursued with vision, faith and courage, and as such it is a heartening lesson which carries its own inspiration of confidence and hope for the future.'
Thomas Twistington-Higgins, from a book celebrating the centenary of Great Ormond Street Hospital in 1952

With such an illustrious past, Great Ormond Street Hospital has a lot to live up to. It has earned its excellent reputation as one of the best children's hospitals in the world over more than 150 years. During that time, it has consistently shown itself to be an innovative and pioneering institution, dedicated to its central mission to treat sick children. It has also been, as this book has shown, a place of extraordinary events and remarkable people, significant breakthroughs in medicine and astonishing stories about both children and adults.

The hospital's future will be built on its reputation not just for the best possible medical treatments, but for attending to all the needs of patients and their families

A successful present

This golden era for Great Ormond Street Hospital remains undiminished. As scientific and medical knowledge have improved, and as a comprehensive healthcare system has developed in Britain in the form of the NHS, so Great Ormond Street Hospital has achieved ever more effectively its primary goal of treating as many sick children as successfully as possible. Improvements in drugs, technology and diagnostic methods, coupled with the benefit of collaborative and globally disseminated research, have made the clinical outcomes for the children treated at Great Ormond Street Hospital the best they have ever been.

Furthermore, the hospital has since the Second World War focused increasingly on creating a therapeutic environment to benefit children not merely clinically but on every level. It is this emphasis on looking beyond a child's medical condition, to their overall wellbeing and that of their family, that has come to characterise Great Ormond Street Hospital's approach today, and which informs its vision for the future. There is every reason, then, for the hospital to have a very optimistic outlook, firmly rooted in its considerable historical achievements.

A bright future

Perhaps the most tangible part of the future of the hospital will be its new buildings. These will help it to provide more child-friendly surroundings, which are relaxing and reassuring as well as being of the highest possible clinical standard. The expectation is that the redevelopment of the hospital will ultimately enable it to treat 20 per cent more NHS patients a year, in much better facilities. Martin Elliot, a cardiac surgeon at the hospital, emphasises the need for these new facilities:

'Modern medicine requires more than just a bed. When Great Ormond Street Hospital was originally designed, that was perhaps enough. But not now. We want to treat our patients to the best standards in the world; the standards they deserve and their parents expect. We are struggling to do that in the buildings we occupy now, let alone in the future as technological advances expand what we can do and the quality with which we can do it.'

Architecture for the future

The design of phase two of the redevelopment programme at the hospital is the responsibility of architects Llewelyn Davies Yeang. The company has been designing hospital buildings since its foundation in 1960 by Richard Llewelyn Davies and John Weeks. Of course, the name of Llewelyn Davies is familiar to Great Ormond Street Hospital, since the Llewelyn Davies boys were the inspiration for JM Barrie's characters Peter Pan and the Lost Boys in *Peter Pan*. There is a link here: Richard Llewelyn Davies, by remarkable coincidence, was a cousin of those boys.

Architecture can have a profound impact on people's lives, and this is reflected in the breadth of the considerations taken into account during the design process in a major project such as this. The vision developed between the hospital redevelopment team and the architects encompasses a number of different aspirations, based on various needs which the final buildings will, it is hoped, ultimately fulfil. These range from value for money to making a positive contribution to the area's built environment in general. One major component of this vision is to create a healing environment on a densely developed, inner city site. This significant design challenge is made more demanding still by the fact that planning restrictions limit building heights on Great

This vision of the new street frontage of the hospital on Guildford Street being delivered in the second phase of the redevelopment programme provides clear public expression of the hospital's commitment to modernisation and innovation

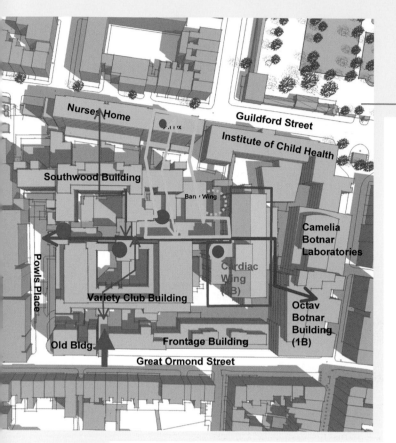

Nurses Home

Guildford Street

Institute of Child Health

Southwood Building

Barc Wing

Camelia
Botnar
Laboratories

Cardiac
Wing
(3B)

Variety Club Building

Octav
Botnar
Building
(1B)

Powis Place

Old Bldg.

Frontage Building

Great Ormond Street

The delivery of further phases of the hospital's redevelopment programme will modernise its facilities, improve the overall user experience and allow better delivery of its core services

The role of the arts

The arts strategy for the new building is central to the overall design concept, and links with other issues about the quality of the interior space and navigation through it. Art has often been seen merely as an added extra in buildings – literally 'paintings on the wall' – but here it is being fully integrated from the outset. Works of art will help to create a friendly, patient- and family-focused environment, and will also be key in enabling people to find their way through the building, and in giving patients a sense of familiarity with their surroundings.

Art will also continue to play a role in the hospital in other wholly non-architectural ways, which contribute to children's wellbeing and development. One excellent example of how the arts and modern computer technology have combined to achieve these aims is in a project devised by music specialist and researcher, Nick Pickett. Thanks to Nick, many children with severe disabilities can enjoy and play music while they are at the hospital.

Nick's work exploits modern technology to offer children some control, choice and fun, all of which are essential to their development and

Ormond Street. Viewing corridors in London protect the view from key sites such as Parliament Hill on Hampstead Heath. This further limits the space in the new build, posing more creative challenges.

The hospital's vision for the future also emphasises sustainability and biodiversity. Technologies such as passive ventilation and an on-site combined heat and power plant will enable the hospital to develop a building legacy that it can be environmentally proud of.

wellbeing. Many of the children Nick works with have had a tracheotomy and are unable to blow out large amounts of air. He has therefore designed a system of air-sensitive devices which can emulate mouse buttons through breath control or air pressure from the mouth. With the help of IT magazine *PC Format*, and the charity Friends of the Children of Great Ormond Street, Nick has combined these devices with infrared technology to enable physically impaired children to play music simply by looking at different points on a computer screen and using their breath action to produce various sounds. Nick has written a number of computer programmes to further develop this idea. One programme, for example, allows children to produce the sounds of different instruments in a marching band, while another presents a picture of a piano with keys that light up as the child looks at them, and which play when the child blows into a mouthpiece.

This is just one example of a non-clinical service provided at the hospital which is of immense benefit to the patients and can, in fact, have a critical impact on a child's quality of life. It also points to the way in which

technological solutions will no doubt continue to have an ever-increasing presence in Great Ormond Street Hospital's future.

Schooling

More conventionally, perhaps, the hospital has provided formal schooling to inpatients since 1951. This has enabled many children to keep up with their schoolwork while undergoing treatment at the hospital, and this often brings a much-needed sense of normality back into their lives. From a single member of staff at the beginning, to thirty-three staff including teachers, teaching assistants and administrators in 2007, the hospital school has undergone enormous change in providing this essential service. The job brings special challenges which would not ordinarily confront a

Children's needs at the hospital are not just medical needs – mental and physical stimulation are an important part of their care and recovery

Banging the drums! Getting better is not about medical outcomes alone. Music is one of many things which can help children to enjoy life after receiving some often extremely intensive treatment

teacher, such as not knowing each week who is going to be coming to their classes, and having to cope, as other members of staff in the hospital do, with the fact that some of the children are not going to get better.

Schooling at the hospital is also undergoing change, driven by the potential of new technologies to extend its reach, both within the hospital and elsewhere. All new non-intensive care beds have their own bed head monitor, creating a 'virtual learning environment' which gives children who are too ill to get out of bed access to learning and entertainment resources. They can even maintain contact with their home schools, to ensure greater continuity of education. John Sosna, an assistant head teacher at the school, says that 'it is hugely stimulating for children to be able to access learning materials from their hospital bed'. It also allows them to be linked up to 'real time events' taking place in the hospital school, such as readings or performances. This technology forms part of a 'blended' approach; it does not replace the contact with teachers, but augments it and provides many new opportunities for addressing the overall needs of children at the hospital.

Pain assessment

It is sometimes difficult to know exactly what the needs of children are, because children cannot always articulate them in a way familiar to adults. This applies particularly to the youngest patients, who have limited language skills. This in turn has an impact on some fundamental aspects of their care – for example, knowing how much pain they are feeling and responding appropriately. Linda Franck, a professor of children's nursing research at Great Ormond Street Hospital, completed a major piece of work on implementing the best nursing practice for pain assessment. Pain assessment is obviously an essential part of the pain management process, and research has shown that when routine, standardised nursing pain assessment is implemented, patients receive improved analgesia (painkillers), experience less pain and are more satisfied with the care they receive. Valid, reliable and developmentally appropriate pain assessment tools are now available for children. Franck's work aimed to disseminate best practice in using these tools, not only at Great Ormond Street Hospital but in children's hospitals around the world. Her work has been vital in instituting the best nursing practice for pain assessment at the hospital.

The National Service Framework

Nationally children's health needs, and the standards of services catering for those needs, have become far more strongly and clearly articulated thanks to the work of Sir Al Aynsley-Green. He has developed a National Service Framework for children, young people and maternity services. When he first started work on this framework, in 2001, Sir Al, who is currently the children's commissioner for England and Wales, was the Nuffield Professor of Child Health at the UCL Institute of Child Health, University College London, as well as the director of clinical research and development there. This major project set out to improve the healthcare being provided to children across the country. Writing at the launch of the framework in 2004, Sir Al explained its importance. These ideas reflect many of the key thoughts on healthcare at Great Ormond Street Hospital:

'For the first time the framework has given clear standards for the care of children in hospital. I'm proud of the way it looks at the holistic approach to the care of children. The three key principles are child-centred services, the whole child and needs-led services. The standards will define the care that children will receive in hospital, the service received and the quality of the environment. It's all about the child actually becoming much more involved in its management and about making sure that every trust has a written policy for the management of pain and use of medicines in children. It's putting children on the radar – children don't have the vote that older people do.'

The vulnerability of children in general, and sick children in particular, means that the right systems have to be in place to ensure they get the best possible treatment

Giving children a voice

Empowering children is evidently a key part of this framework, and this is something that Great Ormond Street Hospital is working towards implementing fully. Children will soon be able to participate in job interviews for some clinical staff at the hospital, for example, and children over ten years old are being invited to become members of the hospital when it becomes a foundation trust. These forms of enfranchisement will ensure that children actually have their own voice in the way things are done at the hospital. This is an enormous step for childhood services, one which would have been unimaginable to the Victorian founders of the hospital. Creating forums where children can articulate their own needs should enable Great Ormond Street Hospital to become an even more child-friendly organisation in the future.

A foundation trust

As a foundation trust, the hospital will have greater freedom from centralised NHS controls, enabling it to plan more effectively for the longer term and giving it greater flexibility in planning and managing major projects. However, its core commitments and its fundamental nature will remain the same – Great Ormond Street Hospital will still deliver its central work of the treatment of children and research into child health to a world-class standard.

Pioneering research and treatments

The immense level of clinical and research expertise across the hospital, coupled with improvements in its environment and new technologies provided by the redevelopment programme, should leave Great Ormond Street Hospital well placed to continue as a global leader in childhood medicine. There is a huge amount of research activity, across all aspects of childhood health, ongoing at the UCL Institute of Child Health and Great Ormond Street Hospital. This has been boosted by its having been awarded biomedical research centre status – the only such centre for childhood health in Britain. Research continues to provide pioneering treatments and insights into the causes of disease, leading to improved clinical outcomes for patients.

The pace of change is often fast – many procedures are taking place which would simply not have been possible twenty, or even ten, years ago, such as keyhole surgery on the pancreas for hyperinsulinism. Success rates for other operations have also increased enormously, which has allowed more focus for longer-term issues about children's post-operative quality of life. New, non-invasive procedures, such as the Bonhoeffer heart valve, enable the hospital to have as little disruptive impact as possible on the lives of its patients. This is a major goal at Great Ormond Street Hospital. A variety of techniques are used to ensure that children do not have to spend a long time in hospital, without compromising their clinical care. There are two positive outcomes of this – improving the patient's experience, and making the hospital more efficient and able to treat a greater number of patients.

Teamwork

A multidisciplinary approach to certain conditions is becoming an increasingly common feature of the hospital's work. One example of this is the highly successful tracheal

Tahlia Lovegrove

In July 2006 Tahlia Lovegrove received life-saving treatment at Great Ormond Street Hospital. Tahlia was born with an extremely rare disease called long segment tracheal stenosis (LSTS) – her windpipe, or trachea, was so narrow that she could hardly breathe. The condition affects just one in five million children, and Great Ormond Street Hospital is the only hospital in Europe that can treat children affected with it. She was put under the care of leading paediatric heart and lung specialist Professor Martin Elliot and his specialist team, who constitute an excellent example of a modern, multidisciplinary approach to treatment.

In 2001, Professor Elliot and his team revolutionised the way in which this disorder is treated, by both changing the surgical method and bringing together a number of different specialists and healthcare professionals to manage the condition. Previously, many children with Tahlia's condition unfortunately died; the surgery now has an 80 per cent success rate. The pioneering surgical method, called primary slide tracheoplasty, shortens and widens the trachea to enable the patient to breathe on their own again. Tahlia's trachea was particularly narrow, posing a big challenge. The normal size of a trachea is 6–8 millimetres, more than three times the size of Tahlia's at the time of her operation.

Tahlia's surgery took five hours to complete. The days following it were critical, as Tahlia learned to breathe on her own. The operation went well, and despite some initial problems Tahlia's parents, Paul and Alison, were able to take her home to Brighton four weeks later.

Paul and Alison say they have been extremely happy with the progress their daughter has made since leaving the hospital. Although her breathing is not perfect, Tahlia's trachea is much stronger than it was before her treatment. 'We were able to remove her naso-gastric feeding tube by the end of

Just ten years ago, the chances of Tahlia surviving her condition would have been slim

August, and since then she has been able to recover her substantial appetite!' says Paul, who took part in a half marathon and a triathlon in 2007 to raise funds for the hospital. 'It was wonderful to bring her home, if not a little daunting at first. Now that she is off all medication and back to her old ways, we often forget what she has been through. Tahlia is an amazing child and really enjoys life. We could not have wished for a better recovery than she has made.'

service. The tracheal team is a group of health professionals brought together to provide a range of expertise for treating a condition called tracheal stenosis – essentially a constricted windpipe through which children struggle to breathe. They may require ECMO (extra corporeal membrane oxygenation), via a modified heart and lung machine which is usually used to support patients whose heart and/or lungs have failed. It is used as a last resort to keep patients alive until surgery can be undertaken.

The tracheal team includes specialists in ear, nose and throat surgery (ENT), interventional radiology, intensive care, cardiothoracic surgery and physiotherapy. Since it was established in 2001, the tracheal service has become one of the largest and most successful of its kind in Europe and a world leader in the field. It currently treats approximately eighty patients a year who, before the mid-1990s, would most probably have died. Tahlia Lovegrove was one such patient (see page 202). The team, led by Martin Elliot, learn each other's relevant skills so that they are all able to carry out certain procedures and effectively contribute to the overall management of the patient. The outcomes of this approach have been hugely effective, with a patient success rate of almost 80 per cent. There is also a cost saving of more than £50,000 per patient using this multidisciplinary team, rather than the previous referral to an individual consultant. This is one example among many that point towards a future of multidisciplinary approaches.

Handprint on the hospital: through empowering children to have more of a voice in how the hospital is run, patients are getting the opportunity to make their mark on its future direction

A remarkable institution

Great Ormond Street Hospital has a special reputation, one that it has spent many years earning and will spend many more years working to improve still further. The place that this book has tried to describe is an extraordinary institution that, despite all the facts, photographs and testimonies, remains somehow indescribable, because of what it does and how that impacts on the lives of so many children, parents and staff. It is a place of high emotion, of joy and sadness, as well as a place where the most dedicated professionals do their jobs to the highest possible standards.

The hospital also deserves to stand among the great British institutions because of its remarkable heritage and its involvement with many of the most eminent and famous figures in British society over the last 150 years, from Charles Dickens to Diana, Princess of Wales. As Great Ormond Street Hospital moves forward, full of ambition with its rebuilding programme and its determination to remain one of the best children's hospitals in the world, it remains in need of charitable support. From such a position of strength it can help to keep childhood health at the top of the political agenda, and play its part in alleviating childhood suffering not just in this country but around the world. The future for Great Ormond Street Hospital is an exciting one, and one in which its motto will continue to be reflected in its practice of caring for 'the child first and always'.

Index

Page numbers in *italics* refer to
illustrations/captions

Acknowledgements

Great Ormond Street Hospital would like to thank the hospital's patron, Her Majesty, Queen Elizabeth II for graciously providing a message to include within this book.

The hospital is indebted to Linford Christie, Tess Daly and Vernon Kay, Gary Lineker, Fiona Phillips and Amanda Redman for their contributions.

We are very fortunate for Dr Lee Elliott Major to have written the introduction for the book.

The hospital would like to congratulate the winners of the patient's story competition and to thank them for contributing their outstanding stories. They are: Harriet Fulcher (whose father Trevor has also been an enormous help), Emma Lucas, Milly Pyne and Louis Tavare.

A number of other patients, ex-patients and their families very kindly agreed to be involved with this book. They are: Oscar and Alexander Chan and family, particularly Dr Alan Chan, Rhys Evans and family, Janine Goulding, Jamie Kenningham, Tahlia Lovegrove and family, Kirsteen Lupton and her father Martin, Simeon Lynch-Prime and his mother June, and Leanne Pannell.

Geraldine McCaughrean has been extremely supportive of the charity generally and very kindly agreed to be interviewed for the book.

The author would like to thank Andrew Birkin who provided invaluable insights into the life of JM Barrie, while Andrew's generous gift to Great Ormond Street Hospital of many archive materials relating to Barrie's life meant that it was possible for some of these to be readily reproduced within the book.

The Harris, O'Gorman and Weston families have given enormous support to the hospital for many years and very kindly agreed to be involved with this book.

Thanks are also due to:

Children's commissioner for England and Wales, Professor Sir Albert Aynsley-Green; Nigel Bennett (Michael Simkins LLP); Kate Harris (Oxford University Press); David Wyatt, for permission to use his fantastic illustrations of Peter Pan; Robert Ingpen; Colin Webb (Palazzo Editions); Diane Hutchinson (Anshen + Allen); Gardiner & Theobald; Susan Snell (The Library and Museum of Freemasonry, Great Queen Street, London); Sophie Slade (The Charles Dickens Museum); The British Library and publishers and theatre licensing agents; Samuel French in London and New York, for their longstanding collaboration with Great Ormond Street Hospital and Peter Pan.

Also worthy of thanks are:

Coenraad Botha, Stephen Featherstone and Jennifer Man from Llewelyn Davies Yeang; Kipper Williams; David Bailey and his studio manager Iain Mills; Marcus Lyon and Glassworks; Mirrorpix; and Joanna Ling and Katherine Marshall from the Cecil Beaton Archive at Sotheby's.

Of the many Great Ormond Street Hospital and Great Ormond Street Hospital Children's Charity staff without whom this book would not have been written, the author is particularly grateful to archivist and curator at Great Ormond Street Hospital, Nicholas Baldwin, and assistant archivist Dr Andrea Tanner for their encyclopaedic knowledge of the hospital's history and their willingness and enthusiasm for sharing it.

The author would similarly like to thank Christine De Poortere for her sage advice, expertise on Peter Pan, kindness and encouragement on many occasions.

Charity director Charles Denton also deserves special thanks for his consistent support and great ideas with this project. Special thanks are also due to Amanda Holt, Simon Kaston and Harriet Powner for all their hard work.

From the hospital and charity thanks also to: Sonal Amin, Angela Attah, Jo Barber, Paul Barnard, Professor Philipp Bonhoeffer, Nancy Bracey, Alex Brown, Chris Chaney, Sir Cyril Chantler, Dr Jane Collins, Cynthia Conquest, Professor Andrew Copp, Clare Cowley, Stephen Cox, Russell Delew, Professor Carol Dezeteux, Elaine Dodds, Professor Martin Elliot, Judith Ellis, Andrew Fane, Carol Flynn, Rachel Forrester, Dr Bobby Gaspar, Professor David Goldblatt, Mark Goninon, Antony Green, Jake Hayes, Peggy Hayes, Judith Hindley, Tim Johnson, Victoria Jones, Laura Le Cheminant, Sue Lyons, Marcella Mcevoy, Katy McMullen, Melissa Michie, Zahid Mukhtar, Emma Pendleton, Bridget Pepper, Louisa Pharaoh, Laura Redmond, Natalie Robinson, Anna Roche, Angie Scarisbrick, John Sosna, Professor Adrian Thrasher, Melanie Vessey, Dr Paul Veys and Zoë Wilks.

The team at Simon & Schuster and Calcium Creative, particularly Paula Borton and Janet Copleston, have shown a fantastic and infectious enthusiasm for this project which has benefited the book enormously.

On a personal note the author would like to give thanks to his wonderful wife, Bridget, who has been incredibly patient and supportive, and to friends and family who saw and heard little of Kevin for many months (a blessing in disguise?).

A number of books were extremely helpful in the writing of this book and some deserve particular mention. They are Dickens by Peter Ackroyd (Minerva, 1991), JM Barrie and the Lost Boys by Andrew Birkin (Constable, 1979), Mutual Friends: Charles Dickens and Great Ormond Street Children's Hospital by Jules Kosky (Weidenfeld and Nicolson, 1989), Great Ormond Street and the Story of Medicine by Jules Kosky and Raymond J. Lunnon (Granta, 1991), Small and Special: the development of hospitals for children in Victorian Britain by Elizabeth Lomax (Wellcome Institute, 1996), The Case of Peter Pan: Or the Impossibility of Children's Fiction by Jacqueline Rose (Macmillan, 1994), The Child First and Always: Great Ormond Street 1852–1952 by Thomas Twistington-Higgins (Odhams Press, 1952), Inventing Wonderland: the lives and fantasies of Lewis Carroll, Edward Lear, JM Barrie, Kenneth Grahame and AA Milne by Jackie Wullschlager (Methuen, 1995), and Dr Frederick Poynton's personal memoirs. The author is also indebted to the work of Dr Andrea Tanner, particularly her article The Sentimental Hard Sell: Establishing the Idea of the Children's Hospital, Proceedings, "Ospedali e Sanita; Strutture, risorse, modelli gestionali, professioni, politiche", Cicloseminariale Citta capitali Europe', Ecole Francaise de Rome (Rome 2004).

I was unconscious when the car crash happened but I was told I was put on a bed and transported to great ormand street.

The nurses on Tiger Ward are all my friends. I like them and they play with me.

I had lots of bloodtests but soon I didnt mind having them.

I had my first operation when I was a baby.

ard is called Tiger Ward

I went to Great Ormond Street Hospital.

In March 2007 I had a big operation and I had to have a RED frame fitted by Prof. and Mr. D.

GOSH

London